WATTS PER KILOGRAM

USING THE COMPUTRAINER™ INDOOR ERGOMETER TO IMPROVE YOUR PERFORMANCE

RICHARD WHARTON
USA CYCLING ELITE COACH
DALLAS, TX

onlinebikecoach.com

ISBN 0-615-31505-4, ISBN 978-0-615-31505-8

Printed in Dallas, TX USA

In Memory of Charles Kulp:
Client, Friend, Mentor, Brother.
Thank you for so many gifts.

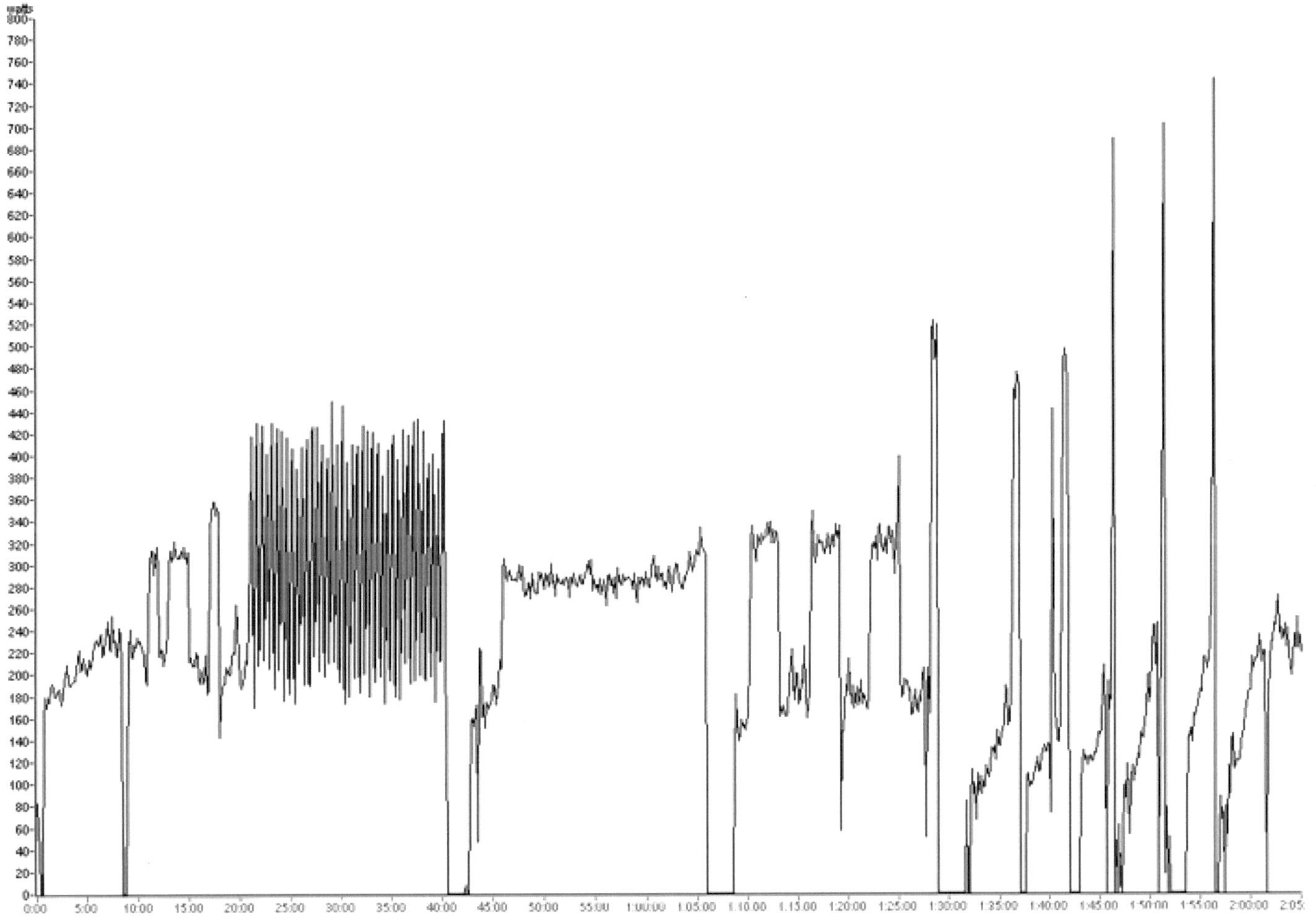

6/29/2004

TABLE OF CONTENTS

ACKNOWLEDGMENTS

Writing this book wouldn't have been possible without the unending support and assistance from several key players:

- My wife, Amy, who has helped me stick with this project through thick and thin.
- Paul Smeulders, the genius programmer who gave me the idea of merging software with a book in order to explain things better.
- Tim Becker, a fantastic coach and supporter from inside RacerMate's offices.
- Roger Moore, the guy who probably knows more about the CompuTrainer than anyone.
- Charles Kulp, who was the most inspiring athlete and client I ever had, and whose memory will linger forever.
- Hunter Allen, who showed me that using technology for coaching analysis and programming really *is* a science.
- Dr. Conrad Earnest, Ph.D., for his pioneering research in exercise physiology and kinesiology.
- Dr. Andy Coggan, for his pioneering research in wattage training concepts, including training stress score, normalized power, and intensity factor.
- Kurt Chacon, nationally recognized expert on biomechanics — and my training buddy.
- Robyn Gregory, my editor and web developer.
- Jay Polsgrove, the first real coach and mentor who ever showed me how to use the CompuTrainer and train effectively with wattage.
- The Mirage Cycling Club of Dallas, Texas — the best bunch of racing buddies I've ever had.
- Frustrated CompuTrainer owners everywhere!

NOTES

For CompuTrainer users only — does not apply to VeloTron users.

FOR PURPOSES OF CONSISTENCY, ALL COMPUTRAINER ROLLING RESISTANCE CALIBRATIONS (RRC) SHOULD BE PERFORMED AT A LEVEL EQUAL TO OR HIGHER THAN 2.0.

In my experience, this is the resistance that yields the best accuracy and consistency. Yes, this will probably tear up your tires, but I feel it's worth $30 every few months to obtain data that's as accurate and consistent as possible with outdoor, real-world rides.

In order to get the most out of your CompuTrainer, I recommend purchasing a hard compound tire like the TACX Indoor Trainer Tire or the Continental Ultra Sport Hometrainer. Soft tires — such as the TACX Blue — don't last as long when used in this manner, thanks to the high heat and pressure placed on them by the CompuTrainer load generator.

Train intelligently, train consistently, and train hard, and you'll get more out of your CompuTrainer than you ever imagined.

I am available via email (info@onlinebikecoach.com) to answer any questions you may have.

- The files that accompany this book are available for download here: http://www.onlinebikecoach.com/WPK/WPK-Files.zip
- The Intellicoach Software can be found here: http://www.cyclingpeakssoftware.com/
- The Goal-Setting software which goes with Chapter 9 can be found here: http://www.single-step.com/
- The latest updates to the Coaching Software and 3-d software from Racermate are here: http://www.computrainer.com/html/coaching_software_support.htm
- Since publication, Intellicoach Erg+ and Real 3d were purchased by Trainingpeaks/ CyclingPeaks. You might think about a package purchase.

INTRODUCTION

Welcome to the world of CompuTraining. By purchasing your CompuTrainer, you have made an important investment which can help you enhance your physiology and improve your performance in all cycling activities. Since the late 1980s, CompuTrainer has set the standard for training with power, and its early use of wattage as a determinant of performance was years ahead of its time. If you use your CompuTrainer wisely, you will be rewarded with more stamina, more efficient riding, more strength in the hills, and more power in the sprints. Think of this purchase as a butterfly's cocoon; soon your metamorphosis will be complete and you will burst out of your basement (or garage, or shed, or wherever your significant other allows you to keep the thing) with more power than ever before.

The workouts and theories presented here represent the absolute latest information available in the fields of exercise physiology, kinesiology, biochemistry, biomechanics, sport psychology, and sport nutrition. You will find that over time your workouts will be of higher quality, will take less time, and will be safer and more effective than those you may have tried before.

Indoor training has shown itself to be the perfect supplement to outdoor riding. It allows you to train specific systems in an environmentally consistent venue. Plus, you never have to worry about ozone, rain, snow, or temperature extremes. By combining your regular rides, cross-training, and races with the workouts included in this manual, you will be able to improve upon three of the four parameters of performance in bicycle competition: speed, strength, and stamina. The fourth — skill — is still best worked on outdoors.

Most of the sample exercises in this book can also be found on the CD-Rom included in the back of the book, or in the ZIP file that comes with the electronic version of the book (henceforth referred to as the CD/ZIP).

Before continuing, you should install the following programs on your computer:

- *CompuTrainer 3-D:* Determine different power averages using realistic resistance and force loads. Pre-ride course profiles from a large library. Free, available on the CD/ZIP or at www.racermateinc.com.
- *CompuTrainer Coaching Software:* Create wattage-specific workouts (.erg files) and convert completed .erg and *CompuTrainer 3-D* workout files into .txt format for your own analysis. Free, available on the CD/ZIP or at www.racermateinc.com.
- *Intellicoach Profiler*: Import CompuTrainer files and assess average power output over different lengths of time. Free (shareware), available on the CD/ZIP.

- *Intellicoach Erg+*: Create custom power protocol workouts for *CompuTrainer Coaching Software* based on actual rides or races for indoor duplication and analyze power readouts from several different sources. The software's creator, Paul Smeulders, has contributed Chapter 9 of this book to help you better understand the power of the *Intellicoach Erg+* application. Purchase through www.trainingpeaks.com.
- *CyclingPeaks*: Assess your workouts by measuring stress and intensity in a practical way. Create wattage training zones and alter them as you get more fit. Upload to the TrainingPeaks website to share the data with your coach. Purchase through www.trainingpeaks.com.
- *Single-Step Motivational Software*: Set your training goals, prioritize them, and stay on track. Purchase through www.single-step.com.

I started writing this book in November 2003 in response to several conversations and web forum discussions about the simultaneous potential of – and frustration with – wattage-based ergometers, specifically the CompuTrainer. One insider commented at the time, "There are over 22,000 CompuTrainer units out there, but fewer than 100 people really know how to use them successfully!" If you're a cyclist looking for better performance, there really is no better way to train than with wattage load resistance and assessment. Despite the idiosyncrasies of the CompuTrainer, it can be the best tool available for you and your training, especially if you're pressed for time.

I began to realize through discussions with clients and fellow CompuTrainer owners that there is more to using the device than just throwing a leg over the bike and pedaling. The CompuTrainer system is an integral part of any training program, and you need to be comfortable with the concepts of progression, periodization, physiological adaptation, training mentality, and properly fueling your body in order for your performance envelope to grow. Therefore, instead of just re-writing the *CompuTrainer Coaching Software* user's manual, I decided to make the book part CompuTrainer how-to manual, part training manual, and part coaching manual.

I try to remain general in the discussions about training and coaching because that's where you (the athlete or coach) have to use your own judgment to make decisions based on the results of the performance tests and foundations that I've provided. Technology and equipment continue to improve our understanding of training and its effects, but decisions regarding the frequency, intensity, and time of your workouts will always be too personal for any non-specific coaching template.

Some of you will already have a high level of experience with the CompuTrainer, and others may be total neophytes or jaded ex-users. So take the chapters as they are, or hop around inside the book and play with the software as you see fit.

I highly recommend the additional investment in an on-bike, outdoor ergometer so you can get data from the real world as well. It will help improve the accuracy and success of your indoor and outdoor workouts, training rides, and even races.

I especially encourage you to try the goal-setting software included on the CD/ZIP that goes with Chapter 10 on sport psychology. Also, Chapter 11 on sport nutrition may be near the end of the book, but I consider it one of the most important chapters.

Finally, this is my first attempt at something so large and detailed, and there will be inevitable typos and errata. Do not hesitate to contact me through www.onlinebikecoach.com with questions, comments, suggestions, or corrections. This is your book as much as it is mine, and you can look forward to updated releases as software and hardware change over time.

Richard P. Wharton

Richard P. Wharton
Online Bike Coach
USA Cycling Elite Coach
Dallas, TX USA

STANDARD WARNING PRIOR TO STARTING ANY EXERCISE PROGRAM

Cycling, while not inherently dangerous, is extremely unforgiving for those who fail to take health and safety seriously. I urge you to see a doctor and get a physical prior to engaging in any sport or exercise. The doctor may not tell you anything you don't already know, but it's always better to be safe than sorry.

If you are new to the sport, if you are not used to long or hard aerobic activity, if you have a family history of Coronary Artery Disease (CAD), if you experience pain in the chest, neck, shoulders, or arms during exercise, if you get dizzy, nauseous, or faint during or after exercise, if you have been diagnosed with high blood pressure, or if you have been told by a doctor that you have *any* type of heart condition, you should talk to a doctor prior to engaging in cycling or any other type of workout.

Chapter 1: THE BASICS OF TRAINING

Cycling is a largely aerobic endurance sport that mixes in bouts of anaerobic intensity and moments where it is only possible to think of endurance in terms of seconds, not minutes or hours. But the key purpose of training with a CompuTrainer is this:

> *"It is your goal to INCREASE YOUR WATTS PER KILOGRAM of body weight as much as possible OVER DIFFERENT AND SPECIFIC PERIODS OF TIME so that you can be better prepared to meet the physiological demands of your sport."*

Paste this mantra onto your PC, your TV, or anywhere else that will help you remember it.

WHAT'S THE BEST WAY TO TRAIN?

In order to optimize watts per kilogram of power output over different periods of time, you need to work on building **stamina**, **strength**, **speed**, and **skill**. To do that, you must manipulate and track the **frequency**, **intensity**, and **time** of your workouts. Workouts should be **specific** to your goals and must progressively **overload** your system over time so that your body will continue to **adapt** to the stress of cycling and become more efficient and strong. You should **periodize**, or coordinate your workouts over the long term to get enough recovery time and help track your overall progress.

Let's break down these very important concepts.

Build Stamina, Strength, Speed, and Skill (The Four S's)

Stamina, strength, speed, and skill are the attributes that make a cyclist better. The main goal of training is to improve The Four S's.

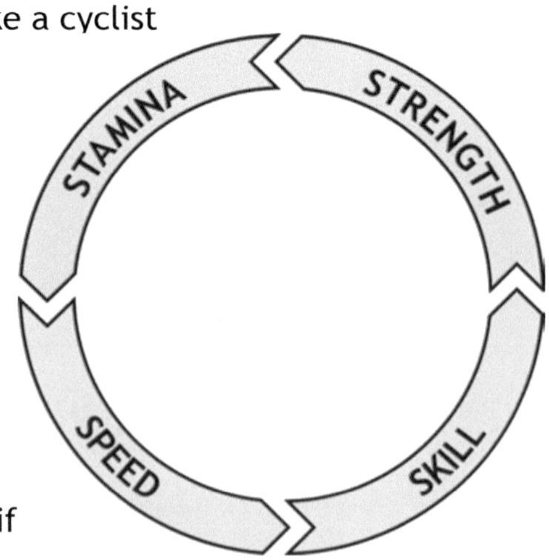

Stamina

Cycling is an inherently endurance-oriented sport. Even track sprinters and BMXers can benefit from some optimization of stamina. Stamina — defined as "enduring strength and energy" — is improved through rides that focus on moderate intensity and progressive overload over extended periods of time. Stamina can be developed through manipulation of the frequency, intensity, and time of your workouts. For instance, if you're working out twice a week, riding 15 miles in an hour, and that's all you ever do, you'll have the stamina to do that and not much more. But if you decide to extend your rides to 25 miles per session and drop the speed or wattage accordingly, then you're working on improving your stamina. Stamina is all about ever-longer distances and the steady progression of endurance. It doesn't always involve riding fast; it's much more about going long.

One of the best ways to improve your stamina on a CompuTrainer is to use the full-screen SpinScan feature in *CompuTrainer Coaching Software*. The SpinScan feature gives you a real-time graphical view of all the pertinent variables on the bike. The visual feedback helps train your brain to fire your muscles in a better way — so instead of having moments of high torque and high drag (this shows up as a peanut shape on the radial graph), your muscles work in a more supple and efficient manner throughout the entire pedal stroke (this creates a graph that more closely resembles a perfect circle).

Now, I warn you: you won't get it the first or second time you try it, but trust me. If you keep training with SpinScan, you'll start to see that your neurological firing patterns shift over time, changing the way your muscles contract and making your pedal stroke as smooth as a turbine engine, allowing you to ride more efficiently at speed than ever. You can save your SpinScan workouts, track the results over time, and witness improvements as the weeks and months progress. You will find more detailed information about using SpinScan in Chapter 8.

Strength

Strength is your body's ability to take a mass — like your body and bike — and move it with ever-increasing force over distance and time. On a bike, strength is what allows you to climb a hill faster or accelerate away from other riders. Strength is built through indoor and outdoor workouts and cross-training activities, like resistance training, and it's one of the biggest benefits you get from training on a CompuTrainer. Building up strength will result in improvement of your wattage per kilogram of body weight over different periods of time more than any of the other Four S's.

A great way to increase your strength using the CompuTrainer is to program intervals at a wattage you know you won't be able to pedal at a regular cadence. Once you drop below the 70 rpm threshold, either practice pedaling at a super-low frequency while seated, or go ahead and stand, using your body as leverage to match the wattage resistance. Doing either of these workouts in five-minute intervals followed by five minutes of recovery will increase your strength, especially in your lower body. If done correctly, it will even help your back and torso.

Speed

Speed is a direct result of both stamina and strength. When your body works more efficiently at lower levels of intensity and stronger at higher levels of intensity, an increase in speed is the only logical conclusion.

Think about a ride you may have been on in which you were able to stick with the group for a while, but at some point you found yourself all alone, spit out the back of the pack like a watermelon seed at a picnic. You didn't fail; you just didn't have the stamina, strength, and speed necessary to stay with the others. Speed can be affected by many physical issues – like aerodynamics and rolling resistance – but it's largely the result of hard work on stamina and strength.

Skill

Skill is the one attribute that CompuTrainer won't help with as much. The CompuTrainer can help you learn how to effectively use a draft to whip around someone and steal a higher finish, but it can't teach you how to bunny-hop, avoid cracks in the road, stay upright when bumped, or read the nuances of a peloton. That's why it shouldn't be used as a replacement for riding outdoors, unless your sole purpose is to get "Compu-fit". "Compu-fit" is not nearly as fit as you would get by going out into the world. Riding outside teaches you balance, ways to handle variable terrain, and how to react to things like traffic lights or animals in the trail. However, the right mix of CompuTraining and real-world training will make you stronger, faster, more efficient, and more skilled as a cyclist.

Manipulate the Frequency, Intensity, and Time of Your Workouts (F.I.T.)

You can improve your stamina, strength, speed, and skill by changing the F.I.T. variables in your workouts.

The frequency of your training is how often you work out (or how often you perform a particular workout). Intensity is how hard you work out, and time is the duration of your workout.

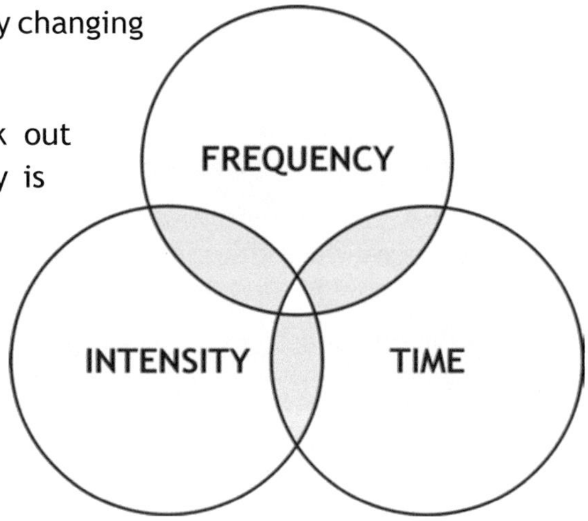

CompuTrainer owners have the luxury of tweaking all three variables, both indoors and out. For what purpose? Remember the workout mantra at the beginning of this chapter. You're trying to increase your performance envelope as much as possible given the other restrictions and limiters in your life.

Make Your Workouts Specific, Overload to Adapt, and Periodize (S.O.A.P.)

Your workouts need to reflect the aspects of your cycling which you want to improve, and they should get harder over time so your body will grow stronger and more efficient. You can coordinate manipulation of the F.I.T. variables over the long term to quantify your improvement.

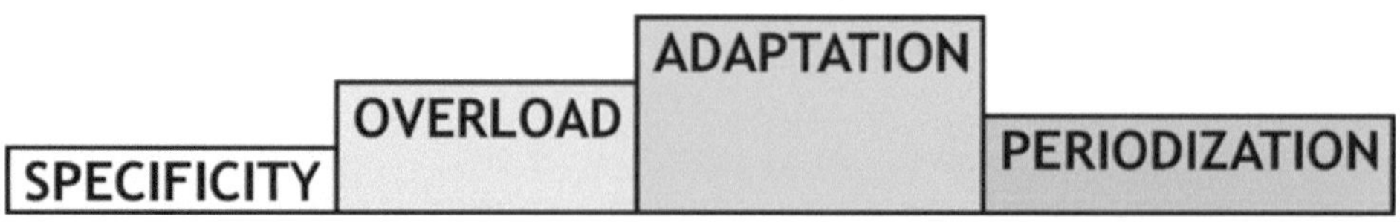

Make Your Workouts Specific

Craft your workouts to focus on the specific demands of your sport (or events within your sport). For instance, recent evidence has shown that mountain bikers have incredibly erratic power outputs over the course of a race on a second-by-second basis. So, in order to train for what they'll encounter in the outside world and to improve performance, mountain bikers might want to focus on short, intense bursts of energy followed by brief pauses to emulate pedaling and coasting through tight and twisty single track.

Roadies, on the other hand, need more aerobic efficiency, combined with efforts above anaerobic threshold two to 10 minutes in length to emulate climbing a hill as they train to attack or bridge up to breaks. Your workouts should specifically address your own personal weaknesses and the aspects of the sport in which you're most involved.

Overload to Adapt

It is essential to engage in what is called progressive overload. Each time you work out, do what you did the time before, but this time do it harder, or for longer. If you continue to do only what you've done in the past, your body will simply maintain the status quo. To improve, you have to keep increasing the F.I.T. variables of your workouts over the long term and push yourself past your current capabilities.

The result of all this specificity and progressive overload will be adaptation. When you stress the different systems in your body, your body responds by altering those systems so the muscles become stronger, work more efficiently, and contract with more force. The next time the same demand is placed on those systems, they will be able to respond with less effort. Our bodies are incredibly efficient machines, and over time we can greatly improve our capacity to do more with less – through adaptation.

Periodize

To make large gains in fitness and prepare properly for competitions, you should coordinate your manipulation of the F.I.T. variables of your training over weeks, months, seasons, and years – taking great care to schedule sufficient recovery intervals. Through periodization you will be able to quantify your short-term and long-term improvements, overload your systems so they respond positively each time you train, and peak at the proper time in your training calendar.

Athletes and coaches have created and followed different generalized modes of periodization for the past 50 years, but with some of the new software that's available, I believe it's possible to micro-manage your efforts and detect trends in power output and physiological and psychological response so you can develop your very own method of periodization – one that is specific to your own capabilities, goals, and structural limitations, such as work, school, and family.

Putting It All Together

The goal of training on a CompuTrainer is to improve your power-to-weight ratio over different periods of time. With an understanding of the concepts discussed in this chapter, you will be able to create a training program that will help you achieve that goal. Remember these concepts:

The Four S's: Build your **stamina**, **strength**, **speed**, and **skill**.

F.I.T.: Manipulate the **frequency**, **intensity**, and **time** of your workouts.

S.O.A.P.: Make your workouts **specific** to the demands of your sport or your weaknesses, **overload** your systems so that the stress forces your body to **adapt**, and **periodize** your training so that you step back from progression every once in a while, let yourself recover, and renew your training with a fresh body and mind.

TRAINING WITH POWER

What do the concepts in Chapter 1 have to do with the CompuTrainer and training with power? When used correctly, the CompuTrainer can be your most important tool. With the CompuTrainer, you can focus on specific physiological demands, programming the frequency, intensity and time of your workouts to progressively overload your neuromuscular and energy systems so they adapt. You can periodize your workouts so you don't over- or under-train, and you can quantify improvements in your stamina, strength, and speed over time by comparing baseline and follow-up performance tests.

Determining Baselines

The first thing you should do at the beginning of any training program is to determine how good you already are. A baseline measurement tells you what level of fitness you're at now, and how to proceed with your training. Since we're training with power, wattage values at baseline are the most crucial numbers. In order to determine baselines for your fitness, we're going to perform some basic tests, and then we'll analyze the results and set your training zones.

There are three baseline tests that I like to perform on athletes. While it is possible to do them back-to-back with adequate recovery, I highly discourage performing more than two tests on one day.

Test #1: The Wingate Max Power Output Test

The first test is designed to measure your maximal power output. To do this, we're going to use the CompuTrainer to determine both your peak power output and average power output over a 320-meter course. For this test, we'll use the *CompuTrainer 3-D* software.

The goal of this test is to go as fast as you can and cover as much ground as possible in the shortest amount of time. This will show you your maximum watts per kilogram and your average watts per kilogram. If you save the resulting file, it will also give you the ability to race against yourself from time to time in order to check your progress.

There is a course on the CD/ZIP with the filename of Wingate_Test.3dc. The course is a straight road about 320 meters long (1,056 feet), set at a .2% incline for purposes of resistance. First, make sure you've got the latest version of *CompuTrainer 3-D*. Start up the program, go to "Build or Load a Course", then click on "Options". If you haven't yet, enter your personal information in the Rider One information area by clicking "New" or "Edit".

Don't forget to add your bike weight to your body weight! Most road bikes, with bottles and saddle bags, are about 20 pounds (9 kilograms), while most mountain bikes with bottles and suspension are about 27 pounds (12.25 kilograms), no matter how much money you spend on expensive lightweight stuff.

After a good warmup of 10-15 minutes, a proper calibration of the rolling resistance (make sure the RRC is set at or above 2.5), and a couple of five-second practice starts, you should be ready to proceed with the test. Set the pacer (if you're using one) at no less than 1500 watts. You want him out of the way. Turn off the Drafting option. Start at a dead stop, in the right gear for fast acceleration, and hit the F1 key. The timer will count down, and when "GO!" appears, start pedaling!

This needs to be a fangs-bared, no-holds-barred, 150% effort. The test will take 25-50 seconds, depending on how much force you can generate. You can do the test standing or seated, and can use any gears you like. Just remember; it's about acceleration, putting out the effort, and then hanging on for dear life as you shoot for the finish line like a rocket car out at the Bonneville Salt Flats.

If you perform the test properly, it is possible that you may get physically sick, so have a barf bucket available, because you may very well throw up or black out afterward due to acute (but temporary) oxygen deprivation, blood glucose shortage, or acidosis.

It also helps to have someone watching, or standing on the CompuTrainer's rear mounts and holding the bike saddle a bit so the device won't tip as you sprint. Even better, follow RacerMate's instructions for building a platform, and bolt the bike stand down to some solid plywood or sheet board. Contact RacerMate (www.racermateinc.com) for those instructions if you need them.

Now, go get recovered, and that means sucking down some carbohydrates, preferably in liquid form. Grape juice or flat soda will probably do the trick, and the soda may settle your stomach. Sophisticated sport drinks also work.

When you've completely recovered, follow the directions in the gray "Saving a Performance File" sidebar on Page 19 to save your file. Name it something like RW_Wingate_Test_YYYY_MM_DD.3dp. Substitute your own initials for the first two letters, and use the current year, month, and date. Then, minimize the *CompuTrainer 3-D* software, open up *CompuTrainer Coaching Software*, and follow the directions in the gray "Converting .3dp Files into .txt" sidebar on Page 20. We'll analyze the results of this test later.

Test #2: Wattage at Vo2Max (wVo2max)

Some time later, when you're completely recovered (at least 20 minutes later, but preferrably after a day or two of rest), get ready for the second test. This test will determine your wattage at Vo2max — your average power output over five or six minutes. I like going six minutes, but in Chapter 3 there's a chart with established parameters put together by Dr. Andy Coggan, Ph.D., which uses average power over five minutes. Either is fine, and the values between the two usually differ by less than 5%.

Using Windows Explorer, copy the 4k_Time_Trial.3dc file from the CD/ZIP into the Courses folder (found inside the CompuTrainer 3D V3 folder). Go back into the *CompuTrainer 3-D* software and load the 4k_Time-Trial.3dc course. The course you are loading is 2.5 miles long and has an incline of .1%. Turn off the pacer, unhook the bike handlebar controller from the PC, and make sure you get a good warmup for yourself and the tire so you can get the RRC calibrated. Make sure the RRC is set at or above 2.5.

After you feel you're adequately warmed up and ready to go, reconnect the handlebar controller to the PC, and make sure the computer is receiving signals. You'll know this is happening when the numbers start to change on the screen as you pedal. Connect the pulse meter to your ear or check to make sure the heart rate monitor is working, and spin up to a good speed. Then, when you're ready, hit the F1 key and start pedaling! Again, this is a fangs-bared, no-holds-barred, 150% percent effort. Only this time, instead of going for about 30 seconds, you'll be racing for 5-9 minutes!

This is no time to pace yourself. You want to ride hard, fast, and strong, and your effort should be reflected in the power output. It will probably drop as you get tired, but don't give up! Everything you need to be doing is in those pedals, and your training future depends on it, so every watt counts!

At the end of the effort, save your file and start your cool-down. You should be pretty well spent. Once you've saved the file (RW_4k_TT_YYYY_MM_DD.3dp, substituting your initials and the current date), exit the *CompuTrainer 3-D* software, go into the *CompuTrainer Coaching Software,* and convert the file to .txt format.

Test #3: Wattage at Lactate Threshold (w@LT)

The final test that you should consider performing is the one that determines wattage at lactate threshold, or w@LT. This test is done to determine how much power you can generate over longer periods of time, and what you need to do to improve your efficiency and speed at and below lactate threshold. Whereas the Wingate Test collects data on your ability to sprint, and the wVo2max test gives you information on how powerful you are in middle-distance bursts, the w@LT test helps determine your aerobic efficiency at speed. It's just as crucial as the other two, and you'll probably use the average w@LT value for more of your training than anything else.

Begin well-rested and recovered from your previous efforts. Using Windows Explorer, copy the 10_mile_TT.3dc file from the CD/ZIP into the Courses folder, and open it up in *CompuTrainer 3-D*. The course for this event is a standard

SAVING A PERFORMANCE FILE

When you're finished with a test, press the Reset button on the handlebar controller (or the R key on the PC keyboard) twice to return to the Build or Load a Course screen.

Click "Save" and pick which rider's performance you want to save. (You can save both rider performance files regardless of whether Rider Two was a pacer or a live rider.)

Type the filename you want to give the race (i.e. RW_4K_TT_YY_MM_DD.3dp), and then click "Save" to copy it to the Rider Performance folder. If you select a filename that already exists, the new file will replace the old one.

10-mile (16.1k) time trial, and it's as flat as a pancake. Unhook the bike handlebar controller from the PC, set the wattage resistance between 100 and 150 watts (smaller riders can make appropriate adjustments to wattage and RRC), and make sure you get a good warmup for yourself and the tire so you can get the RRC calibrated. Make sure the RRC is set at or above 2.5.

After you feel you're adequately warmed up (about 15 minutes), reconnect the handlebar controller to the PC and make sure the computer is receiving signals. You'll know this is happening when the numbers start to change on the screen as you pedal. Connect the pulse meter to your ear, check to see if you're receiving either a pulse from the ear clip or a signal from the heart rate monitor, and spin up to a good speed. When you're ready, hit the F1 key and start pedaling! This effort should last for 20-40 minutes, depending on how efficient you are.

You don't want to be burning up the rubber on your tire in the first five minutes like during the wVo2max test. Instead, pace yourself and try to save the best for last. That doesn't mean you should slack off; 10 miles is like a cross-town commute. It takes a while, and you need to balance speed with efficiency. Still, you should be pretty tired when you're done.

You'll want to race against yourself on this course time after time, so be sure to save the file correctly (use a filename like RW_wLT_Test_YYYY_MM_DD.3dp, substituting your initials and the current date). Also, don't forget to convert the file into .txt format with *CompuTrainer Coaching Software* for later analysis.

Congratulations! You have acquired the most important data that you'll need to improve your performance.

Analyzing the Data

You should now have three data files that will help you determine how much power you can exert over three different time durations.

CONVERTING .3DP FILES INTO .TXT

Saved race files (in this case, anything with a .3dp extension) from any CompuTrainer PC program can be exported as ASCII text files. Go into the *CompuTrainer Coaching Software* (version 1.5 or higher), choose "File", then select either "Export" or change the Export Options if needed.

You will be asked to select the original saved performance file that you want to convert. Then browse to the folder where you would like to save the file. Once exported, the file will have the same name as the original file, but with the .txt file extension added after the .3dp.

Here's what your Export Options ought to look like.

Use a Toss rate of 15 for any files larger than the Wingate Test. You'll still get about two measurements per second, which is more than enough.

Make sure the following boxes are checked: Time, Speed, Power, RPM, Miles, Load, Cadence, Comma Delimited, and Short Format.

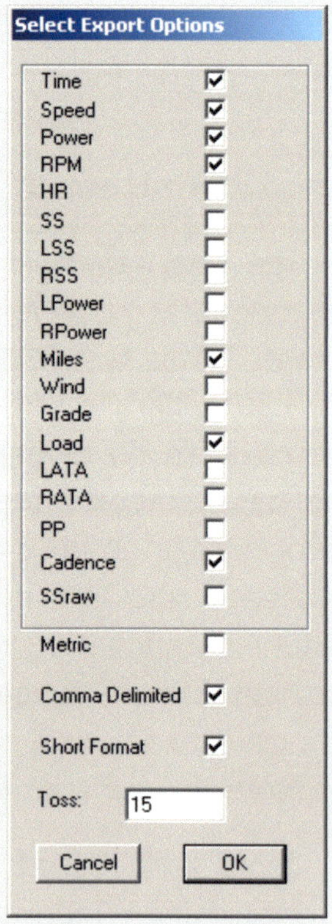

Open *Intellicoach Profiler* 1.0. You'll get a screen that looks like Figure 2-A.

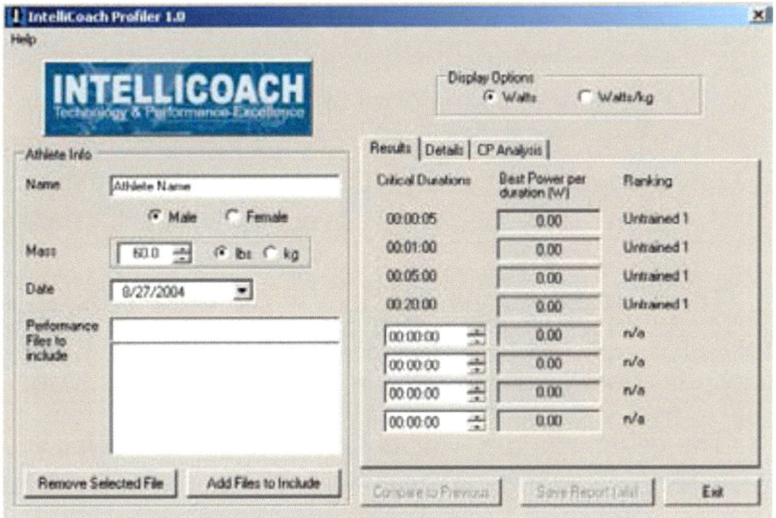

Figure 2-A

Enter your name, your weight, and the date, and click "Add Files to Include". Find the folder where your files are located, highlight each file individually, and click "Open".

If you open the Wingate Test first, you'll get three warning windows telling you that certain parameters in the file haven't been met, but don't worry about them. Those parameters will be filled with the wVo2max and the w@LT files.

Make sure all three test files are in the "Performance Files to Include" window in the lower left. You should see several numbers on the right-hand side of the window (see Figure 2-B).

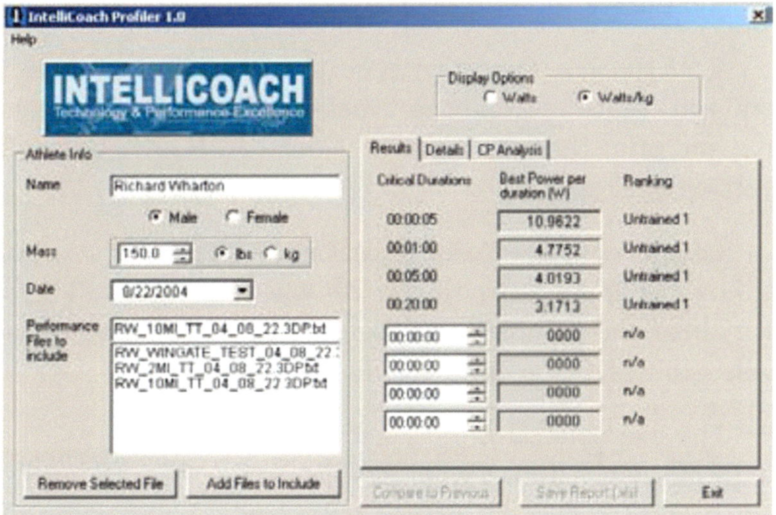

Figure 2-B

The Critical Durations column under the Results tab has four pre-set time durations: five seconds, one minute, five minutes, and 20 minutes. *Intellicoach Profiler* takes the highest average wattage over these durations to help you assess your capabilities. The four pre-set durations correspond with the four primary energy systems your body uses in cycling:

- **Five Seconds:** Roughly corresponds with your body's ability to sprint, generating maximal force in a very short time.
- **One Minute:** Measures your body's ability to perform anaerobically — basically, how much pain and suffering you can put yourself through in a short period of time, like during breakaways (or 1k efforts, if you're an Olympian).
- **Five Minutes:** Measures your body's average wVo2max — the power output required to produce the highest possible rate of oxygen consumption.

- **20 Minutes:** Measures your body's wattage at or slightly above your lactate threshold (w@LT). Lactate threshold is usually defined as the point at which your body stops using the aerobic system for the majority of its metabolic functions and starts to use less efficient methods of energy production. At lactate threshold, the amount of lactic acid you're generating starts overwhelming your ability to process it. If wVo2max is your red line (like the tachometer on a sports car), then w@LT is your body's peak efficiency (the tachometer's yellow line).

There are four blank durations in the Critical Durations column. You can enter any durations you want into these slots, and *Intellicoach Profiler* will display the highest average wattage outputs for each duration, given the data in the files you've included.

The column to the right of Critical Durations gives you the values themselves, either in raw watts or watts per kilogram. As an athlete, it should be your goal to raise these values as high as possible, thus expanding your performance envelope.

The values in the Ranking column should give you a rough idea of how you compare to other cyclists around the world, according to a system devised by Dr. Andy Coggan, Ph.D.

Click the Save Report (.xls) button. This will export the results of your work to an Excel spreadsheet, and will create several reports based on the information you've provided. You may then open the Excel file and print the results for your records. Note: For the file to save properly, you must own a recent version of Excel.

Comparisons of efforts are crucial. When you test yourself to get a baseline value and then undergo training, the only way to confirm whether you are improving over time is to re-test with the same variables and compare your results. (In *Intellicoach Profiler,* click "Compare to Previous" to check watts to watts over the same durations.)

The example shown in Figure 2-C is extreme, but it shows what can happen when you lose weight or improve your performance. By lying to the software that I've lost 45 kilograms (about 100 pounds), my wattage per kilogram critical power (another measurement of maximum sustainable power, similar to w@LT), goes from 3.1 watts per kilogram to 9.1 watts per kilogram, an improvement of 194.12%. Wow!

But back to reality. This feature allows you to compare multiple efforts to see how you're progressing.

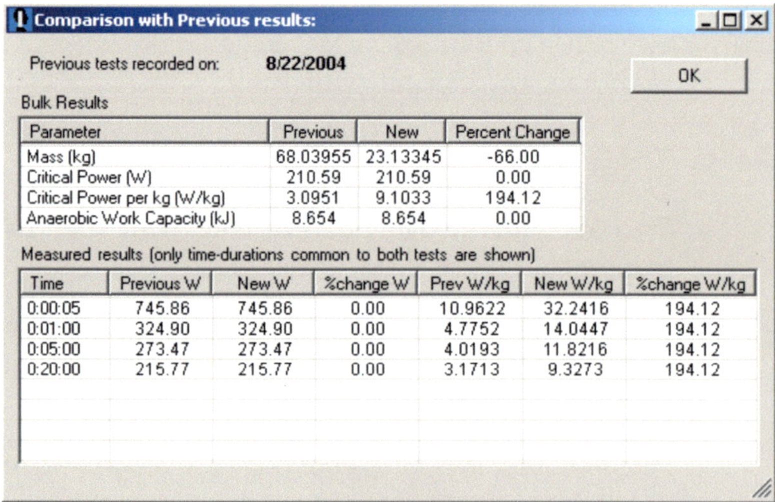
Comparison with Previous results:

Previous tests recorded on: **8/22/2004**

OK

Bulk Results

Parameter	Previous	New	Percent Change
Mass (kg)	68.03955	23.13345	-66.00
Critical Power (W)	210.59	210.59	0.00
Critical Power per kg (W/kg)	3.0951	9.1033	194.12
Anaerobic Work Capacity (kJ)	8.654	8.654	0.00

Measured results (only time-durations common to both tests are shown)

Time	Previous W	New W	%change W	Prev W/kg	New W/kg	%change W/kg
0:00:05	745.86	745.86	0.00	10.9622	32.2416	194.12
0:01:00	324.90	324.90	0.00	4.7752	14.0447	194.12
0:05:00	273.47	273.47	0.00	4.0193	11.8216	194.12
0:20:00	215.77	215.77	0.00	3.1713	9.3273	194.12

Figure 2-C

You now have the four critical baseline values (watts per kilogram over the five-second, one-minute, five-minute, and 20-minute durations) that you need to make training with the CompuTrainer more effective.

You'll want to re-test every six weeks or so in order to check your progress. Be accurate, train intelligently, and you'll be able to quantify changes in your performance. Nothing gives you a bigger confidenceboost than seeing proof that all your hard work is paying off!

Chapter 3: DESIGNING A TRAINING PROGRAM

So you've just purchased this big, expensive training tool, and you don't know how to use it to achieve your goals. Let's look at how to get started with the software and build an overall plan.

We're going to stay away from *CompuTrainer 3-D* for a while, and focus instead on *CompuTrainer Coaching Software*. Why? Distance-based wattage protocols are too variable. Wattage and time-based protocols go a long way toward helping you refine your training. Also, *CompuTrainer Coaching Software* allows you to modify the frequency, intensity, and time (F.I.T.) variables of your workouts, and it helps you improve your speed, strength, and stamina – and maybe some elements of skill, such as sprinting (The Four S's). Not that we won't use *CompuTrainer 3-D*, it's just that those workouts will be secondary to the personalized protocols you can create on your own or with a coach in *CompuTrainer Coaching Software*.

Let's start by opening the *CompuTrainer Coaching Software* and setting you up as an athlete. Click on the Source menu and choose "New". Enter your name, age, body plus bike weight, and gender. For heart rate range, enter 100 (lower) and 200 (upper). You want to set a very broad range for goal heart rate because the CompuTrainer's strength lies in collecting information about wattage, not heart rate or pulse (you'll find more on this topic in Chapter 6). Click OK, and save the user file as "yourname.udf" (substituting your name, of course) so it can be pulled up over and over again. Close the *CompuTrainer Coaching Software* for now; we'll come back to it later.

Take the chart you just created in *Intellicoach Profiler*, and look at where you stand in terms of effort. Looking at my files, it's pretty easy to see that my 20-minute (w@LT) and five-minute (wVo2max) values are okay, but my one-minute (anaerobic capacity), and five-second (sprint) are pretty weak. So do I train to improve upon my strengths or work on eliminating my weaknesses? Why not both?

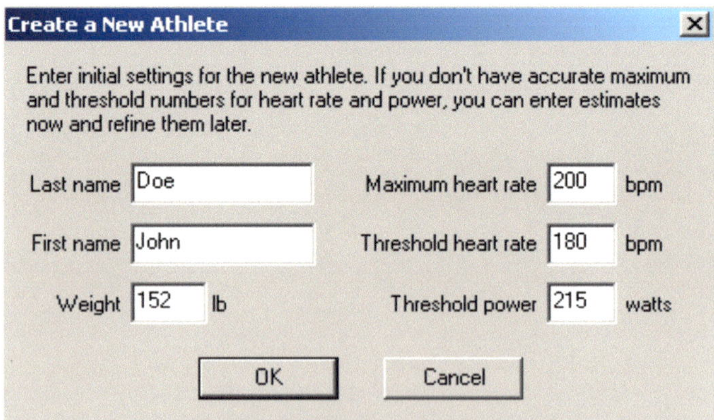

Image © CyclingPeaksSoftware.com

Figure 3-A

Open *CyclingPeaks* and click "Create New Athlete". You'll notice that it asks for both your maximum and your threshold heart rate (see Figure 3-A). For now, unless you already know both your maximum and threshold heart rate, enter 200 and 180, respectively. You can tweak those values later if you want.

Enter your 20-minute w@LT value into the Threshold Power field. My 20-minute average power output is roughly 215 watts, or 3.17

watts per kilogram. By entering that number, I can use *CyclingPeaks* to get some pretty good wattage training zones.

Hunter Allen, a co-creator of *CyclingPeaks*, believes that your true threshold power is probably around 95-97% of your best 20-minute average, but for now I'll stick with the value I got from my baseline tests.

OBTAINING THE TRAINING ZONES

After you click "OK" you will get a screen of several blank charts, one of which outlines some pre-set power training zones and another that contains personal attributes like body weight and the begin and end dates of your season. I'll go into more detail with the rest of *CyclingPeaks* later, but for now the most important thing to look at is the Power Training Zones chart (see Figure 3-B).

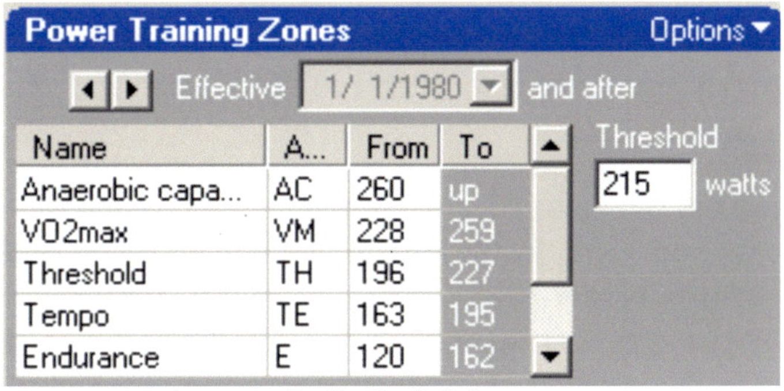

Power Training Zones — Options

Effective 1/ 1/1980 and after

Name	A...	From	To
Anaerobic capa...	AC	260	up
VO2max	VM	228	259
Threshold	TH	196	227
Tempo	TE	163	195
Endurance	E	120	162

Threshold 215 watts

Image © CyclingPeaksSoftware.com

Figure 3-B

The training zones adhere to Dr. Coggan's theory that all training should be based on your current w@LT. The default values are based on the chart in Figure 3-C.

LEVEL	NAME/PURPOSE	% OF WATTAGE AT LACTATE THRESHOLD (wLT)
1	Active Recovery	≤ 55%
2	Endurance	56-75 %
3	Tempo/Steady State	76-90 %
4	Lactate Threshold	91-105 %
5	VO2Max	106-120 %
6	Anaerobic Capacity	121-150 %
7	Neuromuscular Power	N/A

Chart © Andrew Coggan, Ph.D.

Figure 3-C

Write today's date and the values for your power training zones on an index card, and laminate it at your local UPS Store. Place it wherever you can easily see it. You'll use it on a regular basis over the next several weeks to determine what you should be doing. Close *CyclingPeaks* for now. We'll go back to it later, but it's already given us a great deal of information to work with.

As I explained in Chapter 1, training is about performing workouts that are specific to your goals and progressively overloading the body's systems, forcing it to adapt so you can perform better in competitive situations. If competition is not your thing, don't worry; you will get other thrills, like climbing hills faster, finishing metric or English centuries more quickly, and growing more fit in general. Using the CompuTrainer as an integral part of your training leads to all those types of successes. Now that you know your power training zones, your goal should be to train within those zones, adapt to them, and re-test at a later date, in hopes that you can shift those zones upward over time.

This is where the science of coaching and the art of coaching go separate ways. As coaches and athletes, we know that training at certain levels of progression and increasing intensity will yield positive results. However, there's a lot of debate about how much progression is appropriate, how best to periodize training, when to take breaks, and what the proper volume reduction is when tapering for a big event.

I'm not going to try to replace your coach, nor am I going to try to give you some universal template that will work for anyone. Trust me when I say that nothing will direct your training and help you perform better than a certified or licensed coach. Every great athlete in every sport has benefitted from a coach. That said, if you do choose to self-coach, the use of the CompuTrainer in conjunction with *CyclingPeaks* and *Intellicoach Erg+* will help remove some of the guesswork from the process.

This is a good time to think about your specific intrinsic and extrinsic goals. What do you want to accomplish in this sport, and how can you best achieve your goals? Which of The Four S's should you concentrate on improving? How should you manipulate the F.I.T. variables of your workouts? And how do you properly implement the concepts in S.O.A.P.?

If your goal is simply to lose weight and be able to ride farther and faster, then concentrate on improving your stamina and strength rather than skill and speed (I'm using speed here as a relative term for quick actions, like sprints). It's likely that you'll need skill sets that are best learned outdoors, not on a CompuTrainer. The recreational rider or weekend group rider should put more emphasis on the aerobic, tempo/steady state, and threshold zones, rather than on the Vo2max and anaerobic conditioning zones.

If, on the other hand, your goal is to become the sprint queen at the local Tuesday night crit, then concentrate on your speed, strength, and skill. Of course, you will probably see a considerable improvement in your stamina as a result of all the intense training you're going to do.

The examples go on. Mountain bikers in Texas need different skill sets and have different neuromuscular demands than mountain bikers in the Northwest – those "real" mountain bikers need more strength over the distance than the flatlanders do. The Texans need more short-term, immediate speed training and short-burst efforts as they sprint and pedal through the gullies and single track they'll encounter.

In a perfect world, you would undergo baseline tests either at the end of the season or early in the pre-season of the next racing calendar year. You'd take the results of these tests, work on the old-school foundation of base training at low-to-medium intensity and progressive duration, then move on to foundation training that involved steadily increasing intervals of higher intensity, and then specification training, tweaking and tuning your energy systems to optimize everything.

But this is starting to cross the line into explicit coaching and programming, and I promised I wouldn't do that. Instead, let's get you thinking about your own needs. Based on your tests (and previous experiences), you have a pretty good idea of where your wattage baselines are, and what your strengths and weaknesses are. Ask yourself these questions:

Where have you been?

- What is your riding experience (frequency, intensity)?
- What types of rides have you gone on most (intensity, time)?
- How often and how much have you been available to train (frequency, time)?
- What were your goals last week, last month, last season, last year (The Four S's)?

Where are you now?

- What does your ride week look like (frequency, intensity)?
- How many hours and how often are you currently training (frequency, time)?
- What are the other factors in your life right now (family, friends, work, etc.)?
- What is your prime motivation for getting a CompuTrainer and becoming a better cyclist?

Where do you want to go?

- What do you want to accomplish next week, next month, this season, next year?
- How many hours are you willing to dedicate to accomplishing these goals?
- Are you willing to make sacrifices in other areas of your life to help you reach your goals?
- Will seeing a quantifiable difference in your power output per kilogram over different durations help you psychologically achieve more of your goals?

Write down your intrinsic goals. What's it going to take to make you feel better and ride faster, longer, stronger, and smarter? Use the information you've collected in the baseline testing to determine your extrinsic goals. You know what you've done in the past, you know where you are currently, and now you know exactly where you want to be.

Now that we have quantifiable baseline data, it's actually easier to visualize and witness changes in performance. You may want to go through the goal-setting protocol provided in the *Single-Step Motivational Software* to help you keep your goals in mind.

SETTING UP A TABLE OF PROGRESSION

Again, note that I'm not giving you specific instructions for your training. I'm giving you an example of how to use what you've got to lay out *your own* plan for using the CompuTrainer to improve.

Let's use my data from the baseline tests in Chapter 2. Say I have 15 weeks before my first local time trial, an eight-mile affair that goes out across the top of a dam for four miles, has a cone for a turnaround, and returns along the same road. The course is as flat as the engineers could make it, except for a slight climb and descent at the beginning, the end, and the turnaround. The race will be held in the fall, with moderate environmental conditions.

Remember that my 20-minute average power output is 215 watts. I have time to work out indoors three times a week. My body weight (150 pounds) probably will not change much between now and then, and my trusty local bike shop has set me up on my time trial bike, so I know what position will yield the best combination of power and aerodynamics.

In order to improve, I have to increase those watts per kilogram, and I'm not going to do it by just losing weight (in my case, that's not feasible). So, let's set up a table of progression and plan my improvements.

Just to make sure that I know where my lactate threshold is, I set up a series of two 20-minute intervals with a five-minute break in between. Chapter 5 discusses how to build files in *Intellicoach Erg+* for use in *CompuTrainer Coaching Software*, but for now let's assume that I know I can complete two separate 20-minute intervals at 215 watts.

I think it may be feasible for me to improve by 3% per week for several weeks until I plateau. Then I'll probably need a week to lay low and let my body recover from the increasing intensity. Note that while I'm increasing the intensity of my workouts, the frequency and time (duration) stay the same. Figure 3-D shows what I would try to accomplish in the first five weeks of training.

2-by-20s	MONDAY	WEDNESDAY	FRIDAY
Week 15	215	215	215
Week 14	221	221	221
Week 13	228	228	228
Week 12	235	235	235
Week 11	NO RIDE	212	212

Figure 3-D

I programmed a steady 3% per week increase in wattage. After four weeks I adjusted the frequency a little bit by not riding that Monday, and I adjusted the intensity by dropping down to just 212 watts, which is actually below my original set wattage of 215. Hopefully, I've recovered adequately, and my body is ready to undergo some more stress in the upcoming weeks.

2-by-20s	MONDAY	WEDNESDAY	FRIDAY
Week 10	233	233	233
Week 9	240	240	240
Week 8	247	247	247
Week 7	NO RIDE	225	NO RIDE

Figure 3-E

Figure 3-E shows my plan for the following four weeks. Again, I've continued to meet my goals, and the 3% per week increase in intensity is definitely yielding results. I've programmed another decrease in frequency and intensity seven weeks before the time trial, because as you keep adding intensity, you need to add more recovery time. I don't think I can go out and do a 254-watt ride after three straight weeks of progression. I keep the time (duration) the same — 2-by-20s — but I drop the intensity a bit so I can continue to recover and not injure myself or burn out.

This also assumes that I've been able to complete both sets of intervals in each workout. If I had failed on either of the intervals in any given workout, I would have attempted to do that same workout once more. Had I continued to fail to complete the workout, I would have inserted a recovery week and tried again, but if I still failed on either interval after that, I would seriously think about other ways to improve, including abandoning the 2-by-20s and moving on to something else, maybe something shorter yet more intense.

2-by-20s	MONDAY	WEDNESDAY	FRIDAY
Week 6	243	243	243
Week 5	250	250	250
Week 4	258	258	258
Week 3	266	266	266
Week 2	274	247	235
Week 1	NO RIDE	1 by 20 at 274	NO RIDE

Figure 3-F

Now it's six weeks until the time trial (see Figure 3-F), I've improved my 20-minute threshold by 12%, and my legs are feeling pretty good. My back isn't as sore from the new position anymore, and I feel like I've got the inertia to impress myself and others. But I've still got a way to go.

What are the last three weeks in my plan all about? I knew I needed to increase intensity as much as possible, so I skipped the recovery week hoping I could squeeze out those extra watts. On Monday of Week 2 I put all my effort into scoring a new maximum sustainable wattage of 274. Then I started my taper. I did one single 20-minute effort at 274 watts on the Wednesday before the race and then backed off, focusing as much on recovery as possible and riding outdoors at a much lower intensity.

So what's the result? Most important is the confidence you gain from being backed up by quantifiable values. Knowing you can do something — because you have proof that you've actually done it — lets you perform with great self-assurance. And you might even beat that personal record during the race!

If you're looking for quantifiables, look no further than the actual evidence. Just 15 weeks ago, I was a measly 215-watter, cruising along at 3.2 watts per kilogram. Four months later, I was capable of at least 4 watts per kilogram, an astounding 20% improvement. Wow! Just think of the possibilities. I might even be able to break the 20-minute barrier, finishing with an average speed of around 25 mph. By quantifying my improvement in performance, setting new goals on a weekly basis, and confirming that those goals are met by performing the workouts at least three times each, I can continue the progression as much as possible until I plateau. Then I back off, recover, and try again.

WHAT TO DO NEXT

There's nothing more satisfying than accomplishing one goal and setting a new one, and nothing can dash your hopes like repeatedly *not* accomplishing your goals. Failure is as much a part of training as success is; the key is how you handle it. Can't get past 3.5 watts per kilogram on a 20-minute effort? Switch modes — do some 5-by-3s at progressive wattage intervals for a month or two. Sprints not your thing? See if you can improve your Anaerobic Conditioning so you can avoid the sprints altogether.

Eventually, we all reach the limit of the envelope. There will come a time when despite your most concentrated efforts, your gains will be minimal. Athletes in the pro ranks work for months to eke out improvements of less than half a watt per kilogram. And everyone gets burned out at some point. The key to mitigating burnout is keeping things fresh and challenging and knowing when to walk away. Also, do keep in mind that there are so many modifiable and assessable variables that the professional guidance of a coach can be very helpful for your continued growth as a cyclist.

Chapter 4: ALL POWER-BASED TRAINING SHOULD BE STUDIED VIA CYCLINGPEAKS

If you know where you've been and where you are now, you can plan where you're going. I believe *CyclingPeaks* is the most comprehensive, easy-to-use power analysis software available. You can use it with the TrainingPeaks online service to create schedules, upload files for analysis or record keeping, and compare actual vs. planned frequency, intensity, and time of your workouts. You can watch tons of data points and do a lot of great stuff, like:

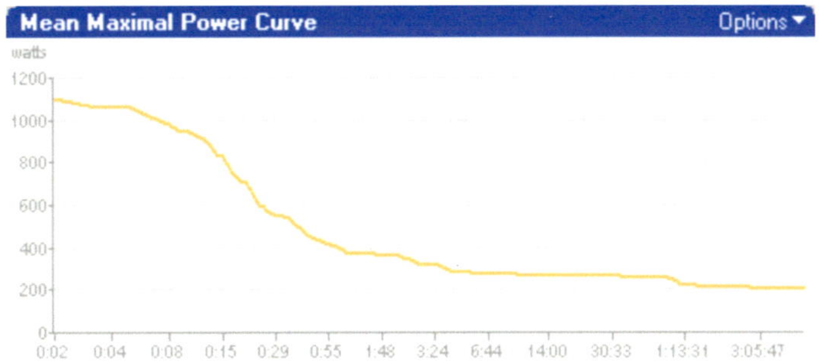

Figure 4-A

- Track average wattage and watts per kilogram from 5 seconds to 20 hours. View the data on any time basis, from daily to annual. Compare one year, week, race, or workout to another. Plan for a peak or realize when environmental factors might affect an outcome.
- Get pre-set peak values on a per-ride basis, from five seconds to 60 minutes. Find intervals within a workout, or answer questions like, "How many efforts started above 350 watts, lasted 12-16 seconds, then dropped below 200 watts?" (Tracking short-term accelerations can help you determine whether to increase intensity, frequency, or both.)
- Measure the performance envelope of a specific ride or series of rides (see Figure 4-A).

Figure 4-A shows a ride in which my mean maximal power for 2 minutes, 48 seconds averaged 286 watts. You can see that the curve slides down as time rolls on.

Figure 4-B shows the same performance envelope over the course of a season. Here, my best power output over 2 minutes, 48 seconds (averaging 329 watts) happened on July 19, 2005.

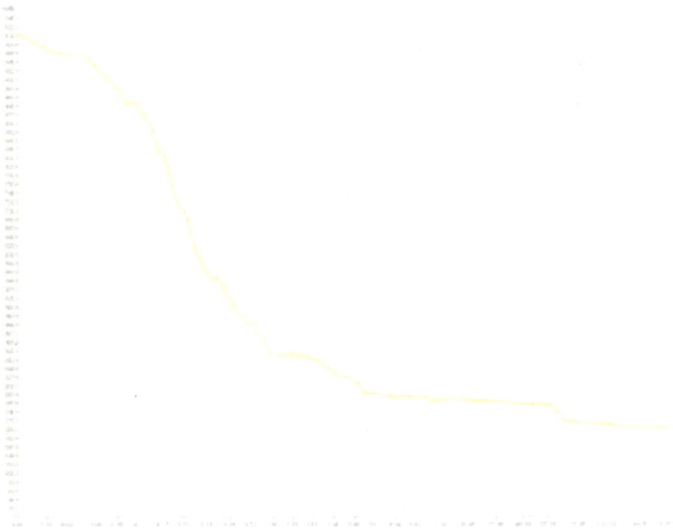

Figure 4-B

Now, here's the cool thing. This graph can be cloned inside *CyclingPeaks*, and then modified to reflect different parameters. If you wanted to look at the 2004 season versus the

2005 season, you would set up the 2004 calendar parameters, clone the graph, then reset the parameters to reflect 2005, and you'd have the two charts side by side. This can be done by day, week, month, quarter, year, whatever. It gives you a clear idea of what you were capable of before and what you are capable of now so you can continue to challenge yourself.

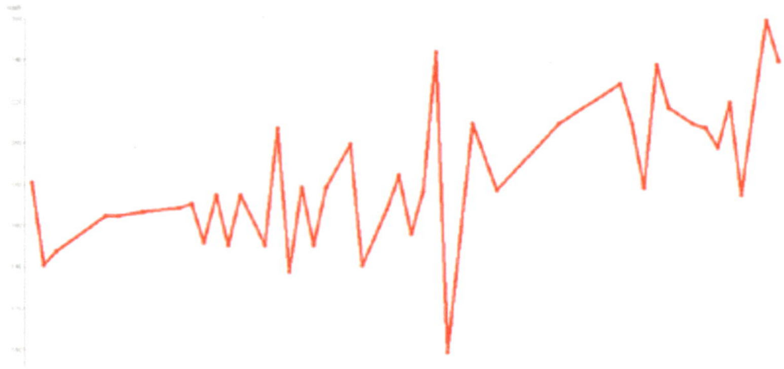

Figure 4-C

Figure 4-C shows six weeks of steady progression of best five-minute wattage average values for an athlete who was focusing on this specific value. It's a combination of indoor and outdoor rides; the two tallest spikes are actually 5-mile outdoor races. Each dot represents one day.

This rider spent several days establishing his five-minute values, both indoor and out, and then worked through intervals on the CompuTrainer to steadily progress and increase his intensity from beginning to end. The first steep peak occurred after a day of relative rest, and the two training days after that were less intense.

Knowing that he had 4 watts per kilogram in his performance arsenal, he went outdoors three training sessions later, pre-rode the race course, and earned a personal record of 4.2 watts per kilogram. He knew he was ready for the event. He recovered the next training session, did a moderate workout indoors at 3.7 watts per kilogram to once again prepare his legs, and then went out and blew the doors off of his personal record, riding at 4.7 watts per kilogram.

Needless to say, he was very happy with his personal record and took a few days off. Then he got back on the bike and started riding the CompuTrainer again, this time progressing from 3.4 watts per kilogram to 3.9 watts per kilogram, backing off, and then hitting it again, matching his indoor personal record of 4 watts per kilogram. About three weeks (10 sessions) later, he hit an indoor personal record of 4.2 watts per kilogram.

CyclingPeaks gives you the information you need in order to interpret how good a performance was, and it does it in a completely customizable and empirical fashion. The graph in Figure 4-C showed just six weeks of data, but it's possible to check progression and periodization of watts per kilogram over four different durations, for as far out as a year and a quarter!

CyclingPeaks also helps you see how hard you worked with the two values they call Intensity Factor (measures the intensity of an interval) and Training Stress Score (measures the metabolic effect of riding at different intensities and different durations on your body). They are valuable methods that help you measure progression and establish daily and weekly goals. With Training Stress Score, Intensity Factor, and another value called Normalized Power, you can quantify changes in your wattage performance and get an idea of how hard a workout was.

The graph in Figure 4-D shows a fairly steady progression over a period of about nine weeks using a seven-day accumulated Training Stress Score. This rider had some major jumps in his training stress during Weeks 4, 7 and 9, which showed when he felt he needed to back off from the previous week's efforts by reducing the volume a bit.

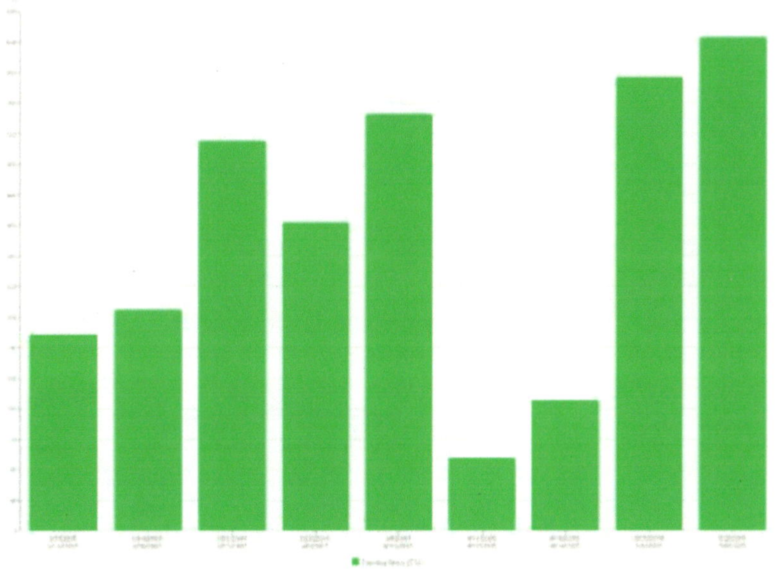

Figure 4-D

I won't go in to all the measurements that are used to make Training Stress Score and Intensity Factors relevant, but suffice it to say that they offer an accurate and quantifiable method of measuring the progression of overall training volume, identifying plateaus, and helping you decide whether you should work harder the next day, keep it the same, back off, or just take a nap.

Furthermore, with *Intellicoach Erg+* you can figure out your TSS and IF score for a particular CompuTrainer workout you've designed before you even attempt it. This allows you to control how often (frequency), how hard (intensity), and how long (time) you need to go to get the training effect you're looking for.

In the next update of this book, I will go into more detail about *CyclingPeaks*, since there is so much more that makes it a valuable complement to training with a CompuTrainer (or any ergometer, for that matter).

Suffice it to say that by performing the baseline tests outlined in Chapter 2, setting wattage training zones as discussed in Chapter 3, and analyzing your workouts and races, you'll be able to create better workouts and progress at an appropriate pace for you.

Based on the chart in Figure 5-A, you can see that my w@LT is okay, but I should probably work on my wVo2max and my five-second sprint power output if I'm ever going to make it out of Cat 4. So let's set up a workout sequence that will work with the wVo2max physiology and help me to improve.

Maximal power output (in W/kg)

	Men				Women			
	5 s	1 min	5 min	FT	5 s	1 min	5 min	FT
	17.24	8.63	5.01	4.18	14.03	7.02	4.30	3.64
	16.97	8.51	4.91	4.09	13.82	6.93	4.20	3.55
	16.70	8.40	4.81	4.00	13.60	6.84	4.11	3.47
	16.43	8.28	4.70	3.91	13.39	6.75	4.02	3.39
Good	16.15	8.17	4.60	3.82	13.17	6.66	3.93	3.31
(e.g., cat. 3)	15.88	8.05	4.50	3.73	12.95	6.57	3.83	3.23
	15.61	7.94	4.39	3.64	12.74	6.48	3.74	3.14
	15.34	7.82	4.29	3.55	12.52	6.39	3.65	3.06
	15.07	7.71	4.19	3.47	12.31	6.30	3.56	2.98
	14.79	7.59	4.08	3.38	12.09	6.21	3.46	2.90
Moderate	14.52	7.48	**3.98**	3.29	11.88	6.12	3.37	2.82
(e.g., cat. 4)	14.25	7.36	3.88	**3.20**	11.66	6.03	3.28	2.73
	13.98	7.25	3.77	3.11	11.45	5.94	3.19	2.65
	13.71	7.13	3.67	3.02	11.23	5.85	3.09	2.57
	13.44	7.02	3.57	2.93	11.01	5.76	3.00	2.49
	13.16	6.90	3.46	2.84	10.80	5.66	2.91	2.40
Fair	12.89	6.79	3.36	2.75	10.58	5.57	2.82	2.32
(e.g., cat. 5)	12.62	6.67	3.26	2.66	10.37	5.48	2.72	2.24
	12.35	6.56	3.15	2.58	10.15	5.39	2.63	2.16
	12.08	6.44	3.05	2.49	9.94	5.30	2.54	2.08
	11.80	6.33	2.95	2.40	9.72	5.21	2.45	1.99
	11.53	6.21	2.84	2.31	9.51	5.12	2.35	1.91
Untrained	11.26	6.10	2.74	2.22	9.29	5.03	2.26	1.83
(e.g., non-racer)	**10.99**	5.99	2.64	2.13	9.07	4.94	2.17	1.75
	10.72	5.87	2.53	2.04	8.86	4.85	2.07	1.67
	10.44	5.76	2.43	1.95	8.64	4.76	1.98	1.58
	10.17	5.64	2.33	1.86	8.43	4.67	1.89	1.50

Figure 5-A

With *Intellicoach Erg+* you can create workouts for use with *CompuTrainer Coaching Software*. Here, we're going to use it to build an interval workout and manipulate the frequency, intensity, and time of those intervals. Open *Intellicoach Erg+* and start a new file by clicking the first icon on the left (looks like a piece of paper with one corner folded over). The screen will then look like Figure 5-B.

Move your mouse to the middle of the graph and click on one of the blue lines. The area on the lower left side of the screen will become active, revealing several boxes and numbers (see Figure 5-C).

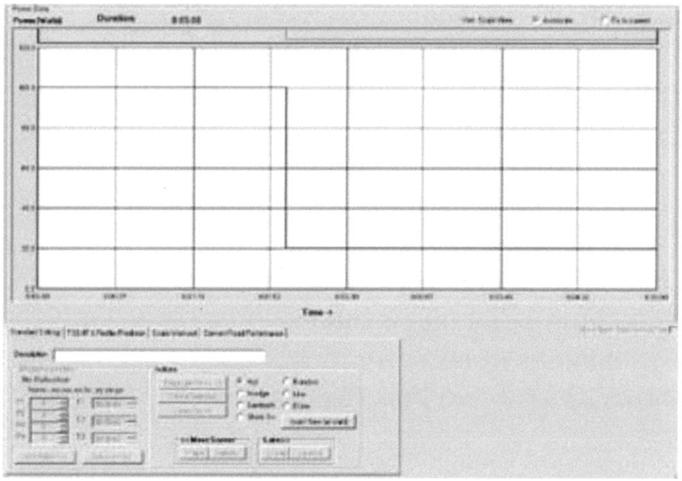

Figure 5-B

The Shape Parameters area has two columns: the P labels (P1, P2, etc.) and their values (in wattage), and the T labels (T1, T2, etc.) and their values (in minutes and seconds). Clicking on the See Definitions button will tell you more about the shapes and clicking on the Set as Default button will set the current shape, wattage, and time values as the default for future intervals.

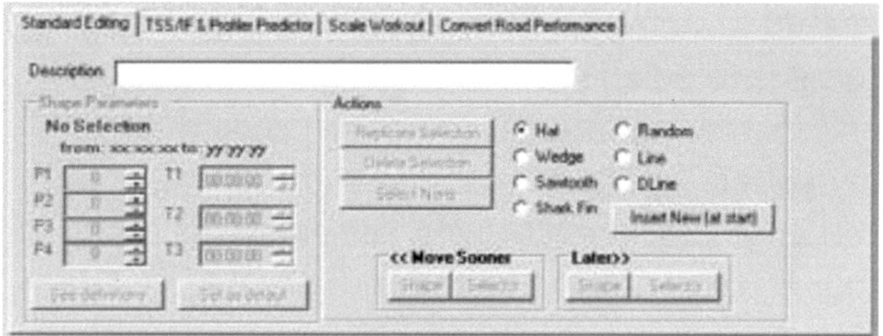

Figure 5-C

The Actions area has several more buttons and shape titles. Most are self-explanatory, but we'll learn more about them as we build the workout.

We know that my wVo2max is about 273 watts, based on the 4k time trial I did earlier. We also know that it's going to take 10-15 minutes to warm up the tire and get a decent RRC at or above 2.5. Unfortunately, the calibration sequence is time we can't record, so keep in mind that the total time we're going to ride prior to the first interval we program here will include the calibration.

The P1 field comes set by default at 300 watts for a period of two minutes. My endurance wattage zone is roughly 120-162 watts, so let's reset P1 as a five-minute warm-up at 140 watts. Now, let's set up P2 as the first interval, with a wattage of 275. This is right at my wVo2max, so I know I'll be panting pretty hard. Let's the time for three minutes, which will be long enough to tax my system, but short enough that I should recover adequately. The Shape Parameters area should now look like Figure 5-D.

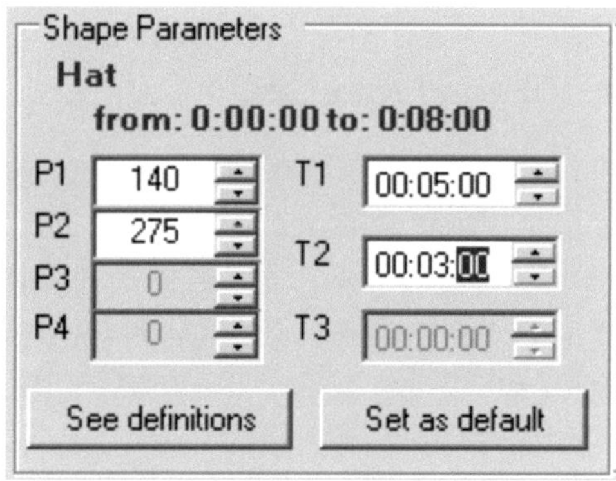

Figure 5-D

Take a look at the main graph area. You may need to click on the Zoom Out icon (looks like a little magnifying glass with a minus sign) near the top of the window in order to get the entire picture, but it should look like Figure 5-E.

Next, look in the Actions area and notice that the Hat button is selected. You should also see the word "Hat" at the top left of the Shape Parameters area. Hat is the simplest type of interval shape. It jumps the wattage of resistance immediately from one load to another.

Let's build another interval similar to this one. Click the Set As Default button, and then click "Replicate Selection". This will add another interval that is three minutes long, with five minutes of recovery time between the two intervals. The graph will now look like Figure 5-F.

Although five minutes is usually plenty of time in which to recover from an effort, the goal of training is to overload one's body and force it to adapt. So by reducing recovery time and increasing interval intensity I should stress my system adequately and take myself right to the edge of failure (which, remember, is not a four-letter word in training vocabulary).

Click "Replicate Section" one more time, then reduce T1 to three minutes. The third interval will look like Figure 5-G. The second recovery time is now shorter, but the durations for all three intervals are the same.

Now let's try and mix things up a bit. Select the Wedge button and then click "Insert New (After Sel.)". Notice that there are now four P labels and two T labels in the Shape Parameters area. P1 is set at a wattage of 250, and P2 is set at 300 (see Figure 5-H).

Change P1 to 100 to make this interval start out at a low wattage. Set P2 at 275, P3 at 225, and P4 at 150. Set T1 at five minutes and T2 at three minutes. Then click on the Zoom Out icon, and take a look at the result. You should see something like Figure 5-I.

This new interval — a Wedge shape — starts

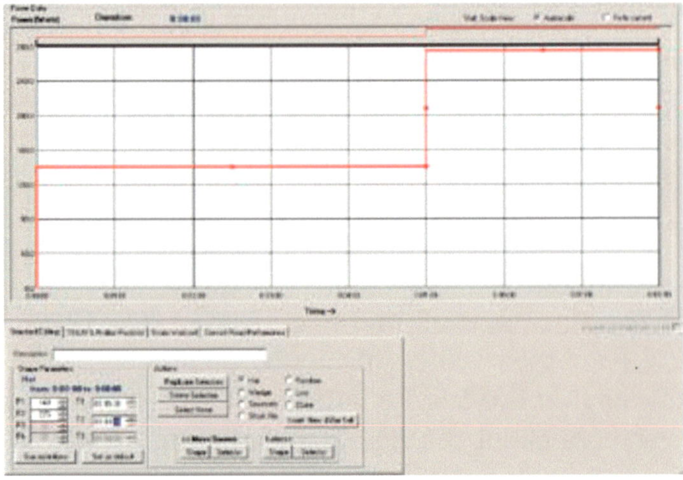

Figure 5-E

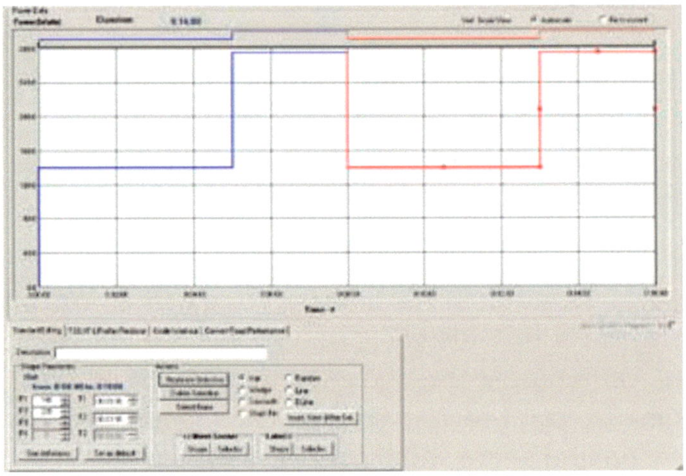

Figure 5-F

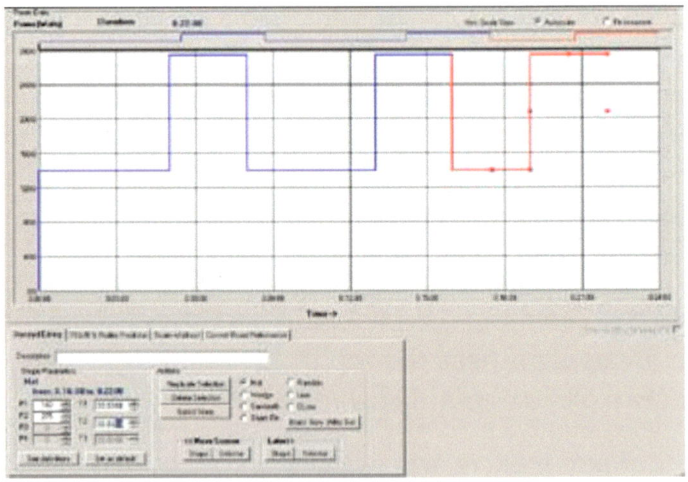

Figure 5-G

at 100 watts and increases resistance until it gets to 275 watts five minutes later. At that point it immediately drops to 225 watts and starts to decrease in wattage for another three minutes until it hits 150.

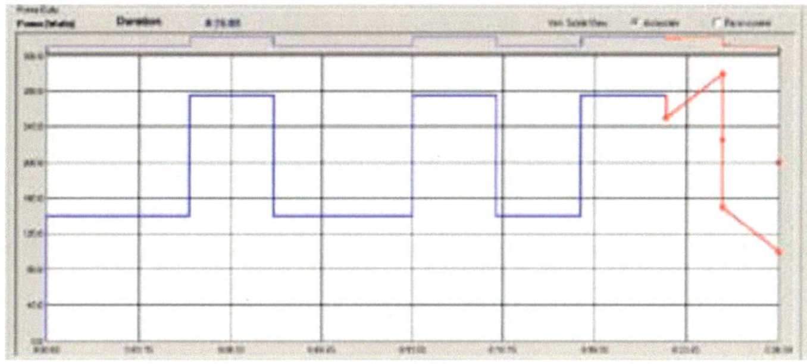

Figure 5-H

Intervals like the kind we just built starts you off easy, increases your effort until you get to a harder wattage, and then keeps the wattage in that same range for a bit, tapering off gently. It's a good interval to do if you want to mimic a surge out on the road. You start off with the pack, subtly increase your speed and wattage, and after a few minutes look to see who's still around. Then you quietly back off and decrease your resistance until you're comfortably back in the pack again.

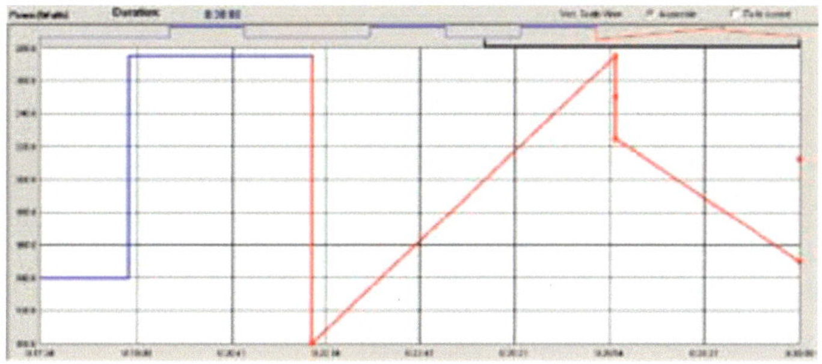

Figure 5-I

So far we have four intervals that add up to a total of 30 minutes of training time. Let's try out the DLine shape next. Select the DLine button and click "Insert New (After Sel.)". After inserting this new interval, the graph will look like Figure 5-J.

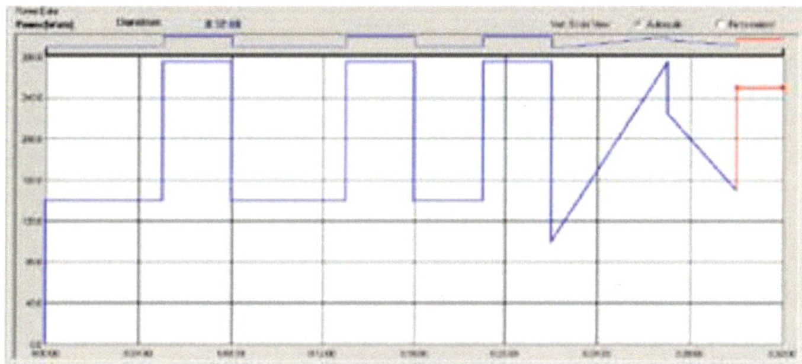

Figure 5-J

After the first four fairly hard intervals I feel I deserve a little easy spinning time. Change P1 to 100, P2 to 150 and T1 to five minutes, meaning that in this interval it will take me five minutes to go from 100 watts to 150 watts. The graph should now look like Figure 5-K.

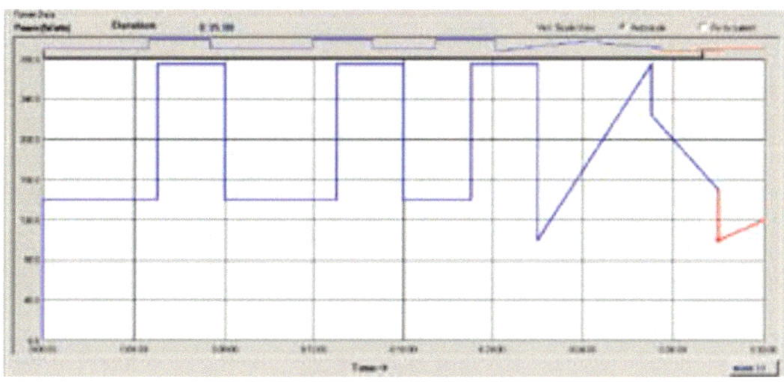

Figure 5-K

One very useful interval shape is the Random shape. Click the Random button, then click "Insert New (After Sel.)". Your results probably won't exactly match mine, but when I added a Random interval, I got a graph like Figure 5-L, and a Shape Parameters area like Figure 5-M.

The largest power spike goes up to 300 watts, and the minimum power over the course of the five minutes is 100 watts. The T2 parameter corresponds to the severity of the wattage spikes. Change T2 from two minutes to one minute, and the wattage spikes get more jagged. Change it to three minutes, and the wattage spikes are less jagged. The T3 parameter deals with the severity of changes in the interval as well, but more on the tail end of the effort, rather than in the middle.

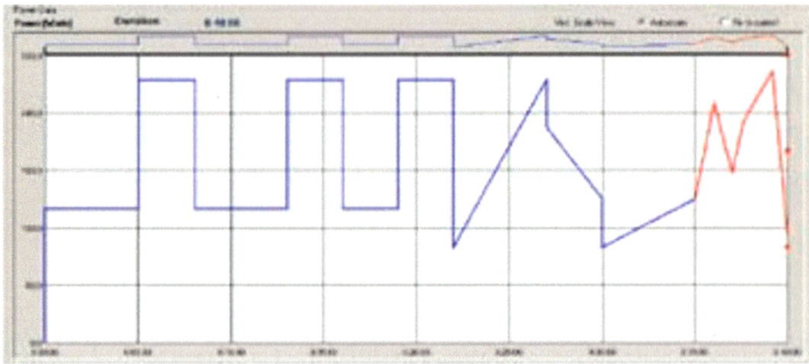

Figure 5-L

We want to keep this interval similar to the first three, yet make it challenging. So let's monkey with the parameters a bit. Set the P and T values similar to the previous intervals' values, using the keyboard and the mouse, and by dragging around the tiny red blocks on the graph itself, and see what turns up on the screen.

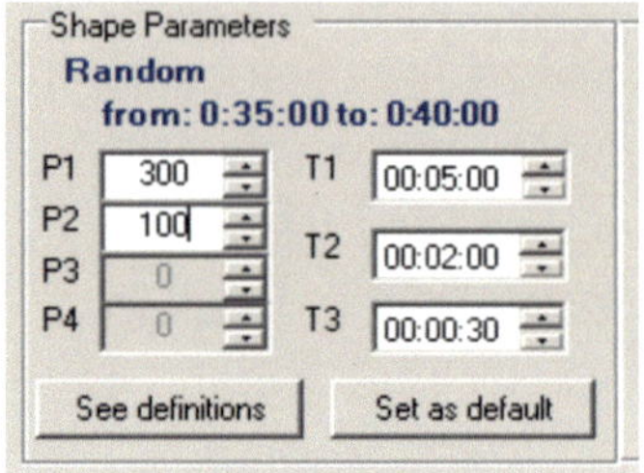

Figure 5-M

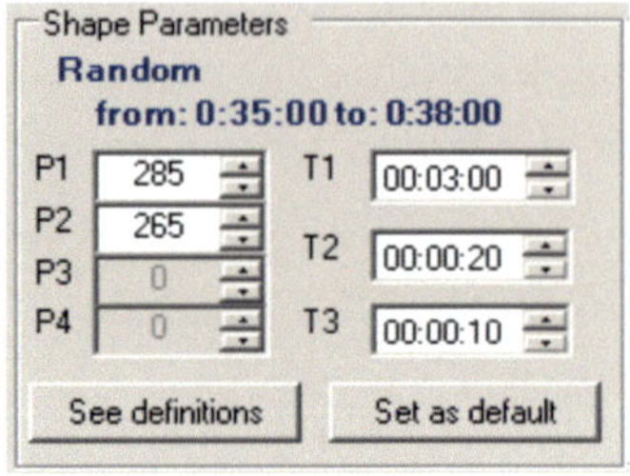

Figure 5-N

I'm going to set my Shape Parameters as shown in Figure 5-N, which will result in an interval that looks like Figure 5-O (I've zoomed in here, using the icon that looks like a magnifying glass with a plus sign). It doesn't look so bad up close, but zoom out a couple of times and it starts to look like the jagged edge of a broken piece of glass (see Figure 5-P).

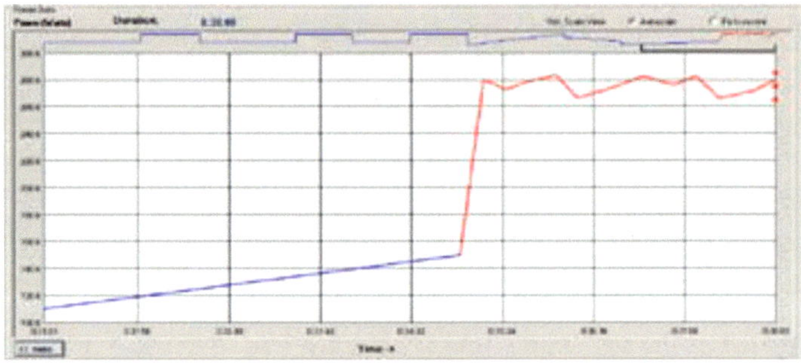

Figure 5-O

The wattage climbs steeply to the allotted wattage range, and then drifts up and down stochastically over the entire three minutes. This is probably one of the most realistic intervals you can come up with, since it mimics what happens out in the real world. Despite our best efforts, we never pump out the watts as smoothly as a turbine engine. It's just not that easy. I highly recommend you use these Random intervals when designing your indoor training plan. The metabolic effects and wattage averages will still be the same as with other interval shapes, but the neuro-muscular training will be much more lifelike.

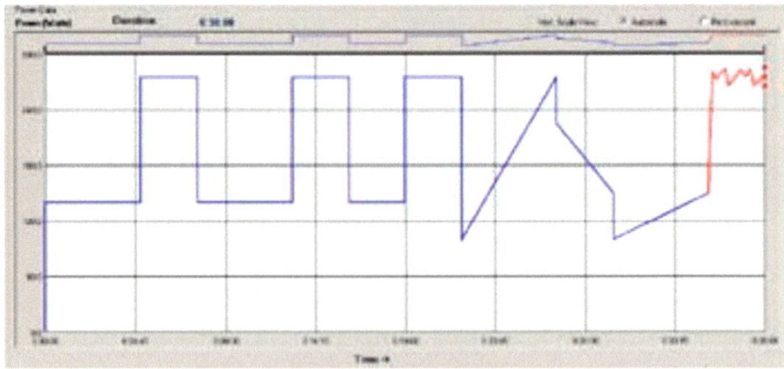

Figure 5-P

Now use what you've learned to create a

recovery period of about five minutes from 100-175 watts. Pop quiz: which shape should you use? DLine. What values should you enter into the shape parameters? P1 should be 100, P2 should be 175, and T1 should be 5 minutes. It's pretty simple!

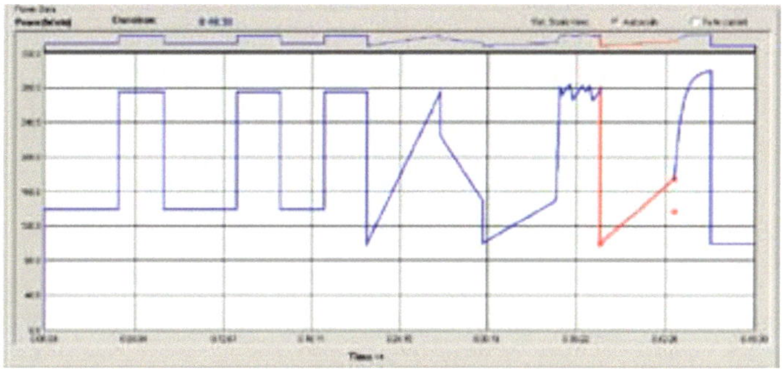

Figure 5-Q

Let's try out another shape. Select the Shark Fin button, and click "Insert New (After Sel).". The new interval will look something like a butter knife (see Figure 5-Q). The Shark Fin is a great sprint simulator. It creates a lot of resistance up front, but the rate of increase in resistance tapers off until it almost hits flatline resistance, and then it drops completely.

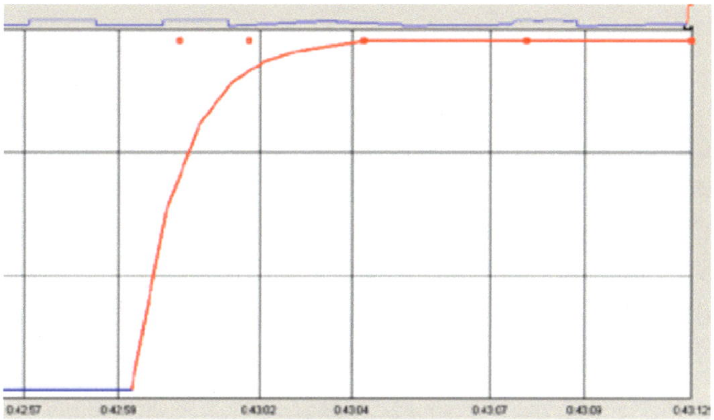

Figure 5-R

Set P1 and P2 at 800 watts, set T1 at five seconds, T2 at seven seconds, and T3 at 00:01 (the steepest setting on a scale of 00:01 to 00:59). The resulting graph (zoomed in) will look like Figure 5-R. We know from the Wingate Test that my best five-second power average is about 745 watts. If I want to improve upon that, I need to be able to accelerate to a maximal power output quickly and then hold on for dear life. So with this Shark Fin interval I'm going to accelerate from 175 watts to 800 watts in five seconds, then hold it at 800 for seven seconds before finally shutting everything down.

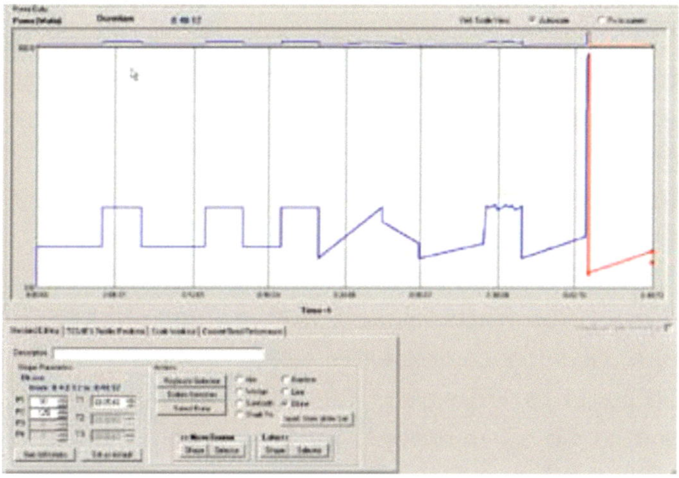

Figure 5-S

The workout itself is done, but I'm going to put one more DLine in there for five minutes from 50-125 watts just to get some recovery time. Figure 5-S is the final graphical representation of this workout. Before *Intellicoach Erg+*, you had to manually enter all the numerical data into a .txt file, but this program allows you to see what you're putting together while you're working on it!

Our workout is now ready to export for use with *CompuTrainer Coaching Software*. Click on "File" in the main menu, then choose "Save Erg+ File" (or, just click the Save icon, which looks like a floppy disk). Type a filename like "Vo2max-Interval-Demo". The workout will be saved as an .erp file, which you can go back and modify later.

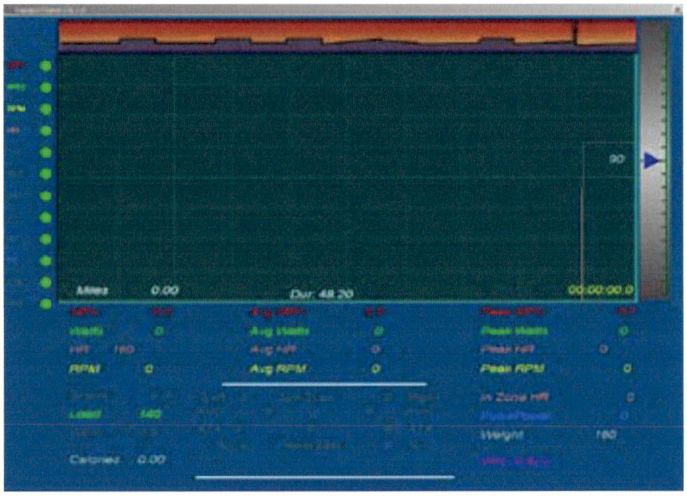

Figure 5-T

To convert the file to .erg format for use in *CompuTrainer Coaching Software*, Click on "File" in the main menu, then choose "Compile to CoachCS Format" (or, just click the icon that looks like a wrench). Make sure you save the file in a folder you can find later. Personally, I like to keep .erp files and .erg files in two separate folders.

Confirm that the file works by opening *CompuTrainer Coaching Software*, clicking on "Charts", and opening the new .erg file ("Vo2max-Interval-Demo.erg"). Hopefully you will see a crude rendition of our graph from Figure 5-S inside the shortened box with the sunset background (see Figure 5-T), along with several numeric readouts in the middle and lower parts of the screen. Chapter 6 is devoted to understanding the *CompuTrainer Coaching Software* screen.

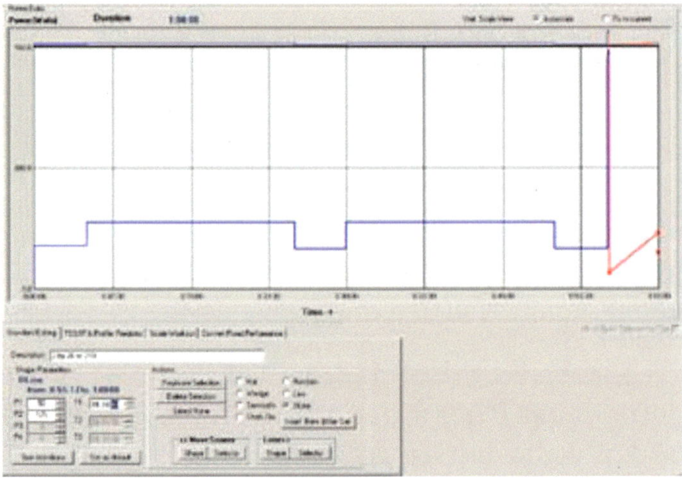

Figure 5-U

It's time to build your own workout. Use *Intellicoach Erg+* to create a workout of 2-by-20s at 210 watts, with a two-minute warm-up at 140 watts, then a five-minute recovery between the first and second intervals that starts at 50 and ends at 150 watts. Add a second recovery period with the same duration and wattage range as the first recovery, then go into a sprint that takes five seconds to ramp up to 750 watts, holds it at 750 for seven seconds, and then drops down to 50 watts. Make the final four minutes and 48 seconds a steady slope upward from 50 watts to 175 watts. The total workout time should be 57 minutes. The final graph should look like Figure 5-U.

We'll revisit this workout in Chapter 7.

I want to take a moment to talk about what you're looking at when you open up *CompuTrainer Coaching Software*. I'll break it down as much as possible, but it's probably worth your while to download and print the official manual for future use. You can find the manual in Adobe PDF format at www.computrainer.com/html/manuals/CTcs15manual.pdf.

Keep "Vo2max-Interval-Demo.erg" (which we created in Chapter 5) open in *CompuTrainer Coaching Software*. The screen should look like Figure 6-A.

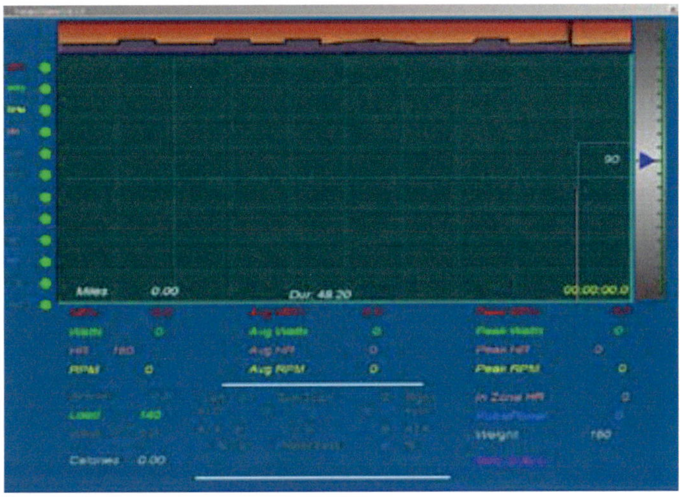

Figure 6-A

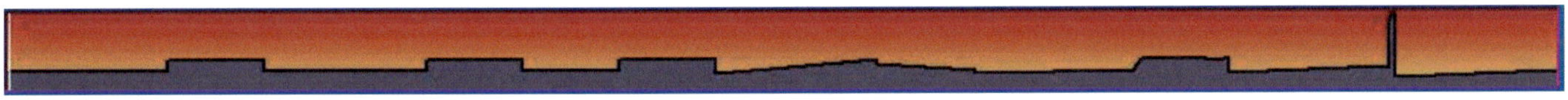

Figure 6-B

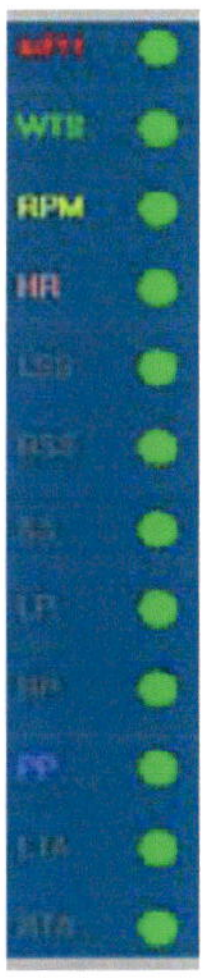

Figure 6-C

Again, the area at the top of the screen (the shortened box with the sunset background) diplays a crude version of the wattage profile we created with *Intellicoach Erg+* in Chapter 5. Figure 6-B shows a close-up view of this area.

When you start performing a workout, you will hit the F1 button on the CompuTrainer handlebar controller. You'll know that the workout is being recorded when you see the yellow numerical clock ticking upward in the bottom-right corner of the main graph. Also, a vertical white line will start traveling from left to right through the top sunset area of the screen to indicate your progress within the workout.

At the bottom center of the main graph you will see "Dur: 48:20", which represents the total duration of the workout (here, 48 minutes and 20 seconds). At the bottom left of the main graph you will see "Miles 0.00", which counts upward as you perform the workout.

The narrow column to the left of the main graph contains several abbreviations, some quite hard to read. Each abbreviation is followed to the right by a green dot (see Figure 6-C). The first four abbreviations (from the top down through "HR") plus "PP" (the third from the bottom) are brightly colored. These are the data points for which measurements will constantly be collected during your workout.

The remaining seven abbreviations should appear grayed out. These data points have to do with the SpinScan feature and are not shown, nor are their corresponding measurements collected during .erg workouts. They are active, however, during terrain-based or distance-based workouts. You will find more detailed information about SpinScan in Chapter 8.

During most .erg workouts you'll see colored lines (corresponding to the abbreviations on the left) moving across the main graph. These lines will show you:

- **MPH (Speed):** You can choose to display speed in Imperial or metric units.
- **WTS (Power Output):** This value is updated about three times per second.
- **RPM (Cadence):** This value is updated about two times per second.
- **HR (Heart Rate):** You can measure heart rate with either the ear clip or the Polar analog receiver; the Polar coded transmitter doesn't work as easily with this system. Be aware that heart rate has always been problematic with the CompuTrainer.
- **PP (PulsePower):** This is a value that CompuTrainer came up with to measure a rider's efficiency by combining heart rate, wattage, and body-plus-bike weight. In theory it works, but there have never been enough studies to validate the protocol, and only recently has the value become available for recording in *CompuTrainer Coaching Software*.

As of this printing, CompuTrainer has released two new CPUs (v 25.43, v 25.45) which are more sensitive to Polar's coded and analog chest straps.You can get more information about CPU upgrades and heart rate monitoring options at Computrainer's forum: http://68.115.203.26/phpBB2/index.php

I do believe that PulsePower could have value in the future, and folks with VeloTrons can use PulsePower more frequently since they come with the ability to receive signals from Polar coded transmitters as well as from analog straps. But for now, I won't dedicate much space to heart rate for lack of a practical hardware solution.

But back to what's on the screen. The narrow column to the right of the main graph contains a gray scale with an arrow centered vertically, pointing to the right (see Figure 6-D). This is a relatively new feature called the RPM Pointer. It's a great tool for those who want to focus on maintaining cadence and wattage during an interval.

Figure 6-D

Prior to your workout, go to "Options" in the main menu and choose "Set Pointer".

Enter your goal RPM and click "OK". During your workout, the RPM Pointer will rise and fall above and below the midpoint, which represents the goal RPM you entered. This helps tremendously if you're trying to achieve and hold a target RPM, especially if you're working on advanced intervals. There is some evidence that a higher RPM makes a cyclist more efficient, and this tool may help you achieve new personal records in wattage.

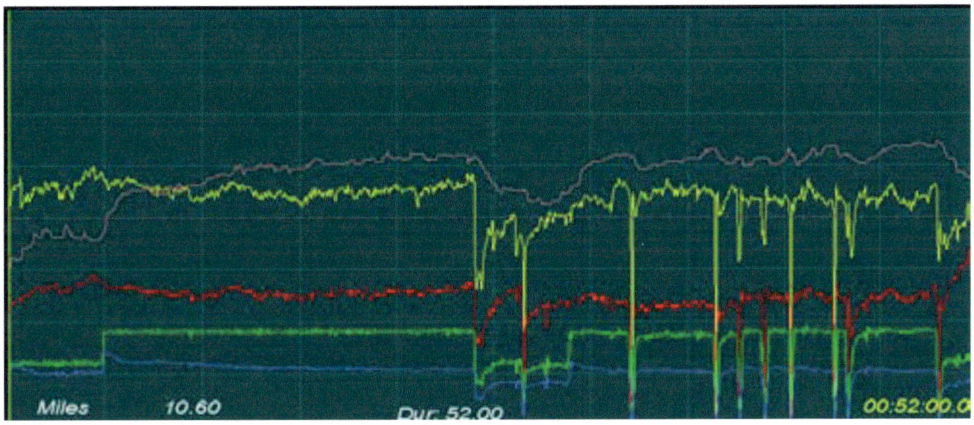

Figure 6-E

I personally don't pay too much attention to the colored lines moving across the main graph (see Figure 6-E). You can increase or decrease the scale to your preference if you want to keep an eye on these lines while you perform the workout, but for me the lines serve the simple purpose of informing me by their motion that the CompuTrainer is still recording. If you're called away from your workout for some reason (phone, doorbell, etc. — heaven forbid!), hit the F1 button on the console to pause the lines while you curse out a telemarketer or accept that Publisher's Clearing House check.

The lower third of the screen displays several great data points, which I feel are more important than the moving lines in the main graph area. Let's take a closer look at these data points in three chunks, from left to right.

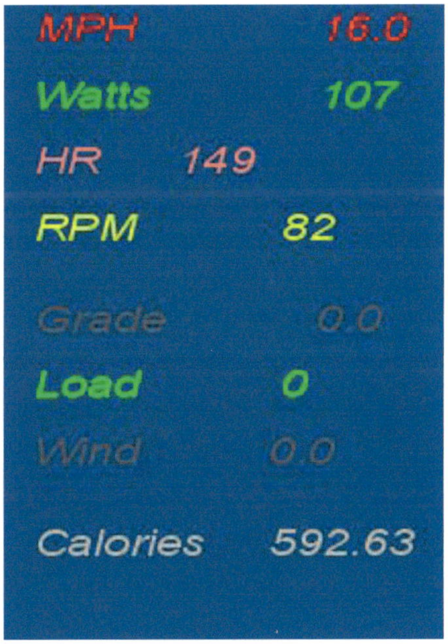

Figure 6-F

Starting with the left chunk, the display shows (see Figure 6-F):

- **MPH:** This one is self-explanatory.

- **Watts:** This value is measured and recorded in real time at a rate around 30 times per second at the tire-cylinder interface. If you feel you want to look at anything on this entire screen, look at the watts value. It's the most important number here.
- **HR:** Heart rate is sort of relevant, but again, due to hardware issues, I wouldn't depend on this value unless you're riding a good VeloTron or have the CompuTrainer CPU v 25.43.
- **RPM:** This measurement is valid and valuable. It gives you an idea of your "happy cadence" – the cadence with which you're most comfortable at different levels of wattage resistance. It also allows you to compare your real-time cadence to your optimal or goal RPM on the right side of the screen.
- **Grade:** This value isn't applicable with .erg load-based workouts, but it could be useful if you wanted to use *CompuTrainer Coaching Software* with a *CompuTrainer 3-D* or *PC Challenge* course.
- **Load:** This is a very important number, perhaps the second most important on the screen. It tells you how much resistance you're supposed to be working against. You want Load and Watts to match. Load is determined by the erg file running the test (it comes from there) and is consistent with it, but if your wattage differs from the load it is due to microaccelerations and de-celerations in your cadence and/or the press on force. If you have 2.5 lbs of rolling resistance programmed into the CompuTrainer, it may actually be the the case that those 2.5 lbs require 125 watts to start rolling the cylinder. You can't have a load and subsequent wattage reading below actual rolling resistance. Contact RacerMate Technical Support if you need further assistance understanding this relationship.

  Note to VeloTron owners: Your load and watts will always be the same due to the wheel and magnet setup. The only way to fail a workout on the VeloTron is to come to a grinding halt and let the interval finish without you.
- **Wind:** This value is not applicable with .erg workouts.
- **Calories:** I'm inclined to believe that this is a calculation of calories converted from actual kilojoules of work (the ratio is something like 1 to 1.1). It may not be the most accurate title for whatever the calculation really is, but it does give a consistent value for overall work based on what's coming out of the wheel into the cylinder.

Moving along to the middle chunk (see Figure 6-G):

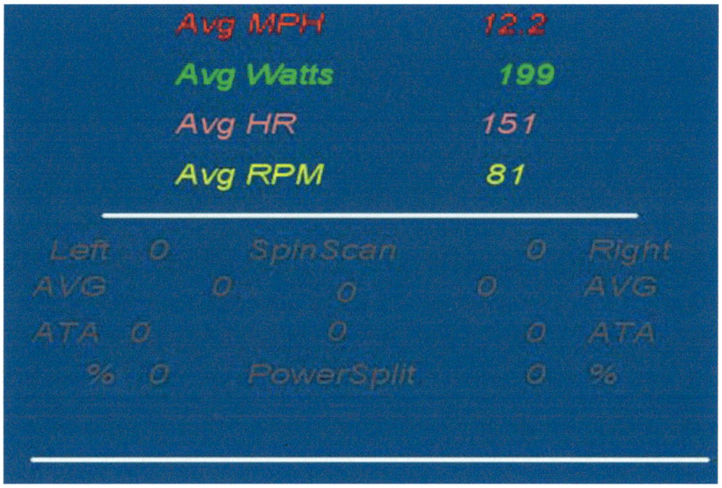

Figure 6-G

- **Avg MPH:** Again, self-explanatory.
- **Avg Watts:** This one isn't as important for an .erg workout, but it could be important if you were using a terrain-based file. It's still interesting, and it's a measurement of overall work, but when you're using different loads on each workout, it just isn't as relevant in the big scheme of things.
- **Average HR:** Not really as important, partly due to hardware limitations, partly due to the fact that we're more focused on watts and load.
- **Average RPM:** I don't feel this is as relevant as real-time RPM. It tracks your average cadence over the entire course of the workout, and therefore can be brought down by any time you spend recovering from intervals. Furthermore, since you're recording real-time RPM, you can look at each interval's average via *CyclingPeaks*, rather than the average over the whole workout.
- **Left, SpinScan, Right, AVG, ATA:** These data points are inactive for .erg files, but available when working with *CompuTrainer 3-D* files.
- **PowerSplit:** This is not available when working with .erg workouts, but the two values (to the right and left of the word PowerSplit) are somewhat important and kind of interesting. These values tell you how much of your overall power is coming from each leg. Ideally, both values would be within three percentage points from 50% most of the time.

  Minor hiccups occur in everyone's pedal stroke, but if you've been through knee surgery or one of your legs is shorter than the other, PowerSplit can tell you how far off you are from pedaling equilibrium and give hints on what to do about it. If you notice one leg truly generating more power than the other leg over an extended period of time, talk to your local bike shop about changing your cleat position on one side, changing saddle height or fore-aft positioning, or even changing the size of one of your cranks. You'd be surprised at what a difference of just 2.5 mm of crank radius can do to equalize power output in a rider's legs. It could also be a great opportunity to get and play with a pair of CompuTrainer VariCranks.

And finally, the right chunk (see Figure 6-H):

- **Peak MPH:** This shows the fastest speed the cylinder went. Speed is not as critical as power in .erg workouts.
- **Peak Watts:** It's nice to have this information at the end of a workout, especially if you're trying to hit a new high on your sprints or something, but for most purposes it's not too important.
- **Peak HR:** Again, heart rate is notoriously inaccurate on the CompuTrainer.
- **Peak RPM:** This one is also nice to know, but it's not as important as all the data points in the left column.

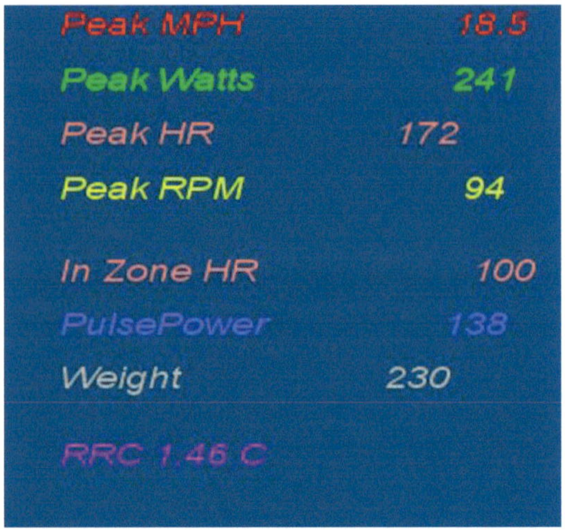

Figure 6-H

- **In Zone HR:** In the beginning of Chapter 3 I had you enter a heart rate range of 100-200. In Zone HR shows the percentage of time you spent in that range. Again, heart rate *is* important, but the CompuTrainer's hardware limitations make it less effective than on more modern devices. Remember, when you're training with power it's all about watts per kilogram per second. I'd much rather have that value displayed on this screen than In Zone HR or PulsePower.
- **PulsePower:** This is a real-time measurement of your efficiency based on power, weight, and heart rate. It's defined as the ratio of watt-seconds per heart beat, or heart energy output, in foot-pounds of torque per heart beat, divided by body-plus-bike weight, times 1000. I think the value has merit, but it needs to be backed up by a white paper study or two and some hardware that measures heart rate better. Until then, I'd ignore it.
- **Weight:** I like having weight displayed, if only to show what little effect one or two pounds of equipment has on a workout. People always ask me how I rank bike weight in importance. I say spend money on good training, achieve your optimal *body* weight, and let the rest take care of itself. Losing 10 pounds will make you faster. Taking one pound off your bike won't do much, unless you're getting paid to race. A final note: Be consistent when adding bike weight. Use changes in body mass to determine how much your performance is improving.
- **RRC:** This is a visual reminder of Rolling Resistance Calibration. With the CompuTrainer use a hard tire, inflated to maximal capacity and calibrated at or above 2.5. The rider in Figure 6-H probably had some wheel slippage at medium-to-high wattage thanks to low RRC.

To summarize, the most important data points to watch while performing an .erg workout are watts and load. Make sure you keep these two close in value, especially when you're doing the interval part of the workout itself. During recovery you can get away with letting wattage dip below the load value, but remember to get back up to speed prior to the beginning of your next interval.

Chapter 7: LOOKING AT WHAT YOU DID, LOOKING AT WHAT YOU'RE GOING TO DO NEXT

At the end of Chapter 5 I asked you to build a workout of intervals that included 2-by-20s and one sprint interval at 750 watts. The resulting graph in *Intellicoach Erg+* should look like Figure 7-A.

Figure 7-A

In order to show off some more of the software's useful features, I had a client perform this same workout. The file he ended up with – "2 by 20at210w1sprint750w.txt" – is included on the CD/ZIP. Let's take a look.

Remember that every workout completed in *CompuTrainer Coaching Software* must be converted from .cdf format to .txt format before it can be read and translated by other programs. The latest versions of *CompuTrainer Coaching Software* and *CompuTrainer 3-D* include an option to convert automatically.

Go into *Intellicoach Erg+* and click on the New File icon (first on the left). Look in the middle of the screen for the Convert Road Performance tab. This function lets you convert any file – including one with data from an outdoor ergometer – into an *Intellicoach Erg+* .erp file for use on the CompuTrainer.

From the Convert Road Performance tab, click "Get Power Meter File". You'll get a screen showing the types of files *Intellicoach Erg+* can currently import. Click "OK". When the file browser window pops up, browse to the CD/ZIP, find "2 by 20at210w1sprint750w.txt", and click "Open". It will ask if you want to remove stops. This is useful when converting an outdoor file with lots of stop signs or red lights, but in this case, click "No". Click "No" again when asked if you want to remove coasting. *Intellicoach Erg+* will import the file and display it in the graph. The result should look like Figure 7-B.

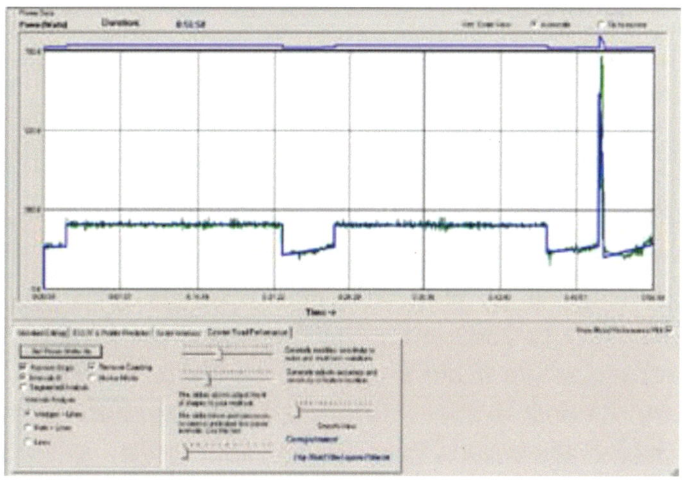

Figure 7-B

Let me point out some things on this screen. First off, the blue lines in the graph are "best fit" load lines based on software parameters, and the green lines represent the actual workout. Beneath the Get Power Meter File button the Intervals Fit button is selected. In the Intervals Analysis area the Wedges + Lines button is selected. At the bottom right of the Convert Road Performance tab, the type of imported file (here, CompuTrainer) and the filename ("2 by 20at210w1sprint750w.txt") are displayed. Below the far bottom right of the graph, the "Show Road Performance Plot" box is checked. And finally, the sliding bars have explanations above and beside them, but don't move them around right now. Let's save that for a more complicated workout.

When I exported the .cdf file to .txt format using *CompuTrainer Coaching Software*, I used a toss factor of 15, which leaves roughly two measurements per second. That is probably more information than we need, but the files will still be small enough to save some disk space.

Click over to the Standard Editing tab, and then move up into the graph and click somewhere on the first interval. The blue line will turn red and the interval's features will be highlighted. Zoom in (use the Zoom In icon or click and drag to create a zoom box) a couple times for more detail (see Figure 7-C). Once you're zoomed in, you can use the More buttons underneath the graph to move left or right.

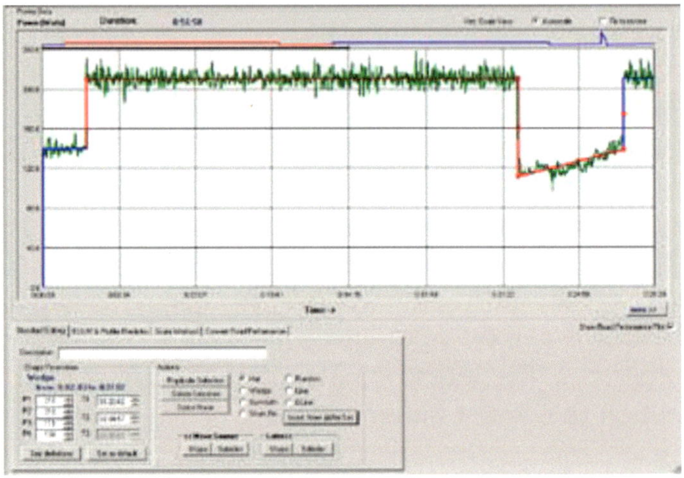

Figure 7-C

Notice that the green workout lines seem to jump up and down a bit more. This really shows the stochastic nature of wattage on a bicycle. I'd say it's highly unlikely that there's anyone who can maintain smooth power output over an entire workout.

In the workout I had you create in Chapter 5, the intervals were 20 minutes long at 210 watts, with five minutes of recovery from 50 to 150 watts. But if you look in the Shape Parameters area for this first interval, you'll see that it went 20 minutes and two seconds at 210 watts, with four minutes and 57 seconds of recovery from 111 to 138 watts. This file is created from actual output from a rider, so all these values are the best fit that *Intellicoach Erg+* saw based on wattage results from the workout itself.

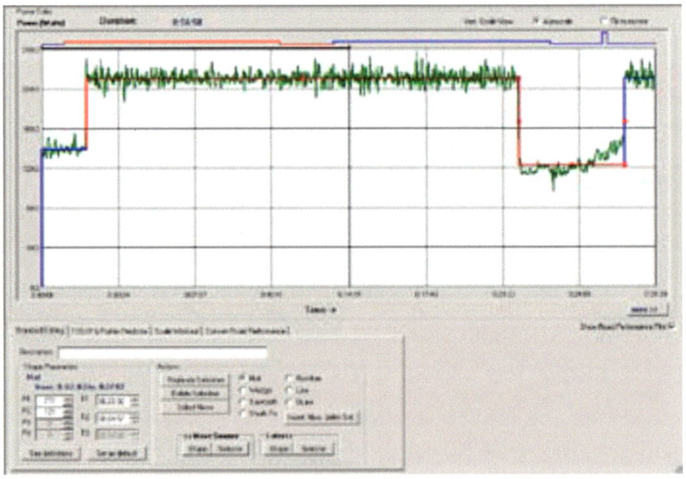

Figure 7-D

Now zoom out until you can see the warmup

and recovery bracketing the first interval. Click back over to the Convert Road Performance tab and select "Hats + Lines" (instead of "Wedge") to make the program see the recovery as a Hat shape instead of a Wedge shape.

Click over to the Standard Editing tab and check the graph to be sure that the best fit line for the first interval and recovery are selected (red, not blue). You will notice that the best fit line for the recovery is now flat instead of sloped (see Figure 7-D).

Click back over to the Convert Road Performance tab once again, and this time, select "Lines" (instead of "Hats + Lines"). You'll get *Intellicoach Erg+*'s best fit analysis (see Figure 7-E) based on the rider's output and certain metrics found on those sliding bars, which we'll get to shortly.

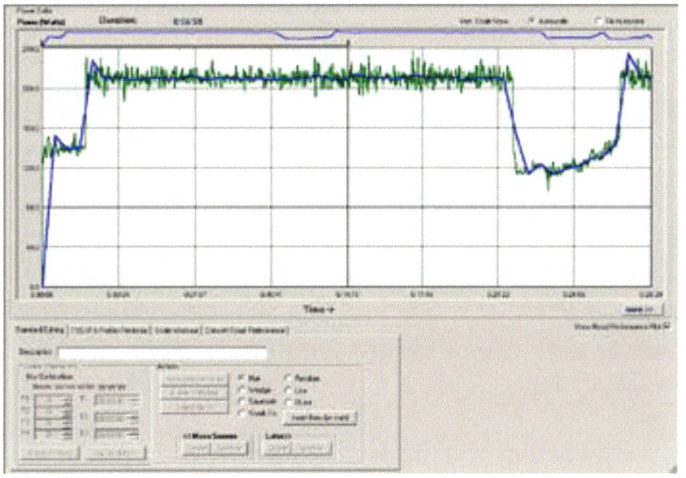

Figure 7-E

The blue load line is now a bit wavy, and it has become really hard to manipulate the entire interval since it's been broken up into so many different pieces. Try it out by clicking back over to the Standard Editing tab and highlighting a section of the blue line. It's now in a bunch of pieces, each about 35 seconds long.

Click back over to the Convert Road Performance tab and switch the selection from "Lines" back to "Hats + Lines" and look at how the top two slider bars in the left column of slider bars — and their definitions — change. It's a bit complex, but it basically boils down to how precise you want the best fit lines to be.

In some cases — for example, when converting a mountain bike race — you might want the best fit lines to be as precise as possible, because in order to improve you have to learn how to pump out more watts in those tiny, crucial segments between trees when the single track is straight enough for you to accelerate and maybe gap a rider on your heels. If you're a more general rider and just want to see what your average power was over a certain period, then you would want best fit lines that are not so chopped up.

Play around with the slider bars later until you're familiar with them and what they can do for your workout. But for now, let's switch back to "Wedges + Lines" and click over to the Scale Workout tab.

In Chapter 3 I showed you how to set up a table of progression, starting with your performance during your best 20 minutes of the 10-mile time trial and scheduling out weekly improvements. With *Intellicoach Erg+* you can self-pace and improve your performance on your own terms rather than based on a template.

The rider that performed this workout was successful in performing the 2-by-20s at 210 watts. So what's next? He can continue to challenge himself by pumping up the intensity – let's say by 3%. Zoom into the first interval by clicking and dragging a zoom box that eliminates both the short warmup and the beginning of the second interval (see Figure 7-F). Select "Only Shapes in Current View Range" in the Time Range to Scale area. In the Scale Factor area, make sure "Percent" is selected, and change the zero value in the box to three. Click "OK + Again". In fact, click it five times. You should get a steady increase in the load line of about 3% (rounded to whole numbers) every time you click. Click back over to the Standard Editing tab to see the monster you've created (see Figure 7-G).

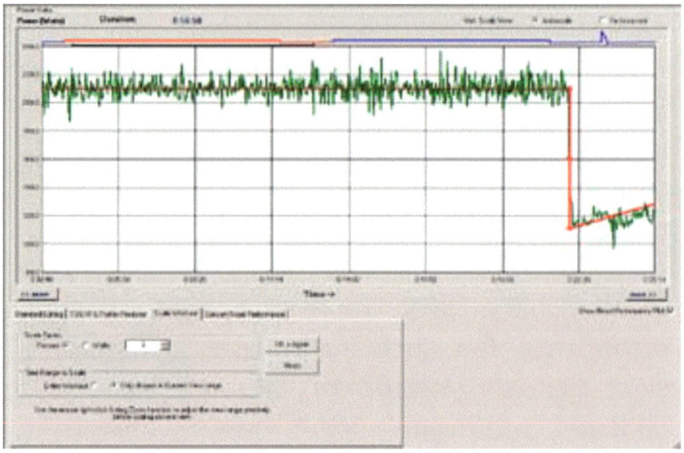

Figure 7-F

By raising the interval intensity by 3% per click for about five clicks, we've taken the wattage on this interval from 210 to 243. That's a little too harsh. Click back over to the Scale Workout tab, click "Undo" four times, and click back over to the Standard Editing tab to see what a much more sane 3% (216 watts) looks like (see Figure 7-H).

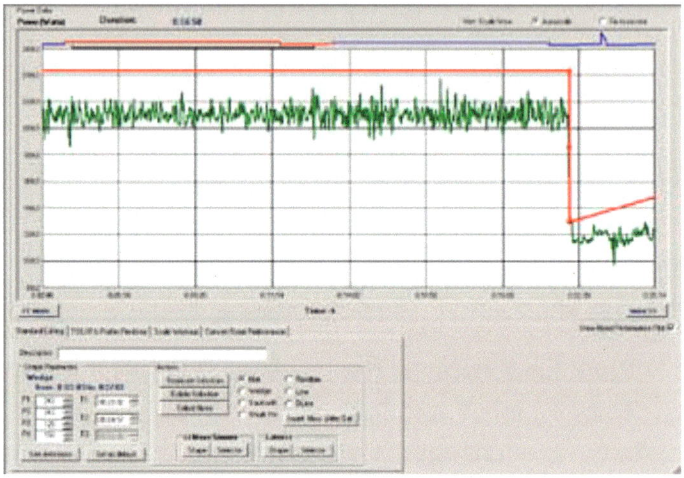

Figure 7-G

Every part of the interval – including the recovery – was manipulated when we did the scaling, so let's use the mouse to manually bring the wattage load of the recovery interval back to the range we had originally created of 50 to 150.

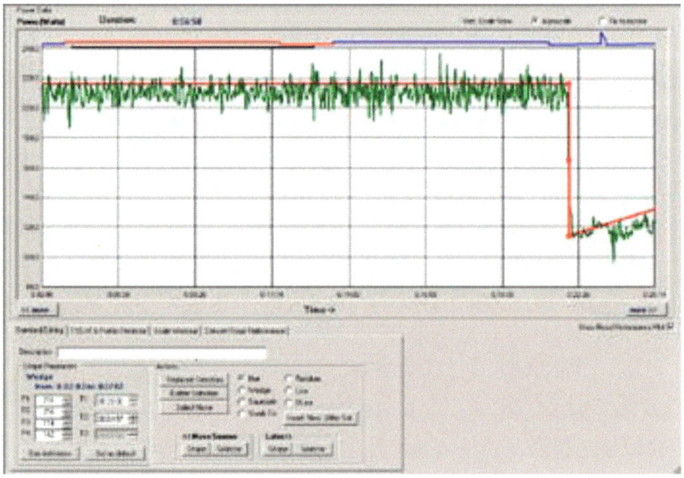

Figure 7-H

Click the More >> button (below the right side of the graph) until you can see the end of the first interval and the beginning of the second interval, with the recovery between. Click on the tiny red square found on the load line at the beginning of the recovery interval and drag it downward until P3 shows 50 watts.

Click and drag the tiny red square found on the load line at the end of the recovery interval until P4 shows 150 watts. The resulting graph will look like Figure 7-I.

Click the More >> button to scroll farther along the graph until the second interval and recovery are visible. Click over to the Scale Workout tab, set the scale factor at 3%, and make sure that "Only Shapes in Current View Range" is selected. Click the OK + Again button once and click back over to the Standard Editing tab. Reset the second recovery interval as increasing from 50 to 150 watts, either by typing values into the Shape Parameters area or by clicking and dragging the tiny red squares in the graph. You should end up with a graph that looks like Figure 7-J.

Click the More >> button again to scroll over to the sprint. We originally built this sprint as a Shark Fin that went from 150 to 750 watts over five seconds at a steep T3 rate of 00:01. Then we set it to hold steady at 750 watts for seven more seconds. Let's compare the pre-planned interval against what this rider actually performed, and then against the best fit load lines *Intellicoach Erg+* created. Figure 7-K shows a zoomed-in view of the rider's performance (green) and the best fit interpretation by *Intellicoach Erg+* (red).

If you were to open the .txt file of this rider's workout in *CyclingPeaks* (see Figure 7-L), you would see that his peak 20-minute average was 210 watts, as expected. But his peak five-second and 10-second averages on the sprint were 759 and 731 watts, respectively.

Perhaps most importantly, take a look at the profile of the rider's actual sprint. It's rounded. It looks a lot like that huge volcanic cone that

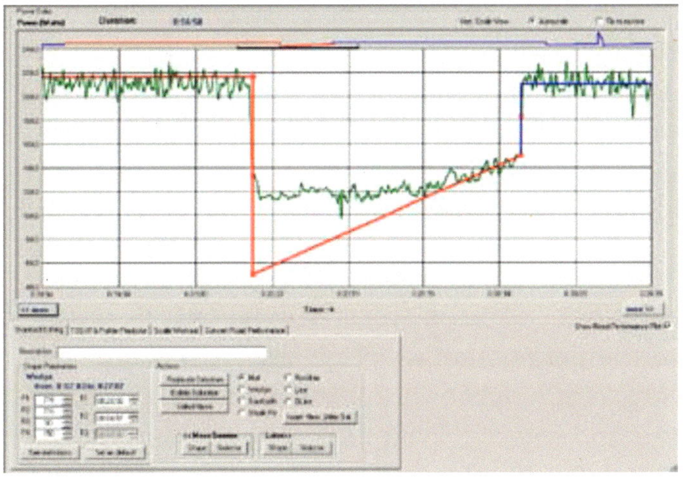

Figure 7-I

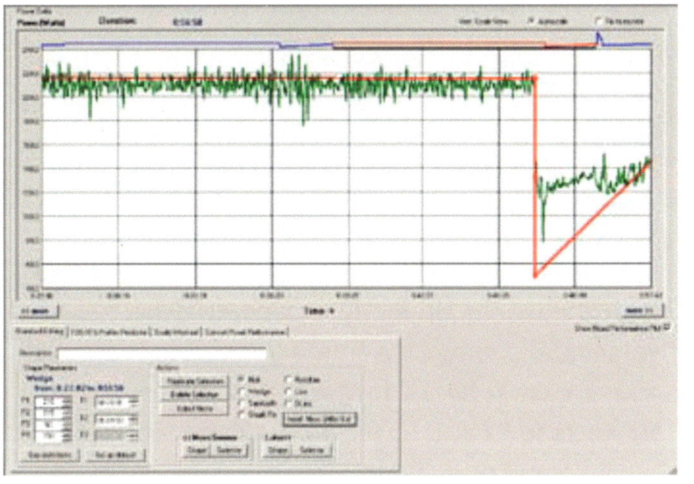

Figure 7-J

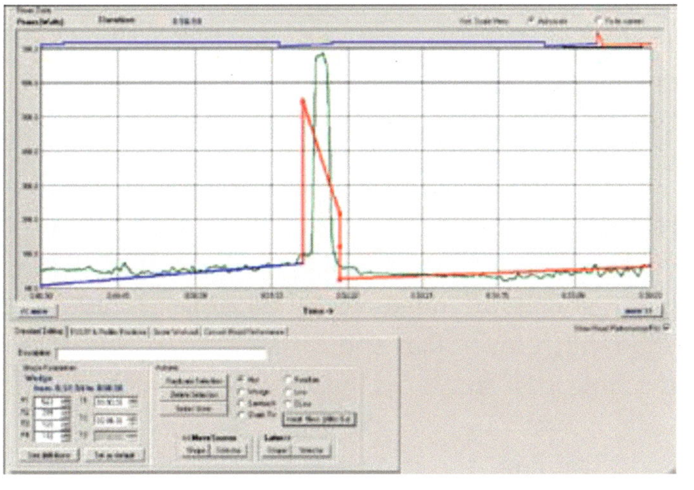

Figure 7-K

served as the backdrop for *Close Encounters of the Third Kind* (see Figure 7-M). The difference between the conical shape the rider produced in his workout and the Shark Fin shape set up in the original .erg file is due to the toss rate of 15, but the actual overlap is pretty close.

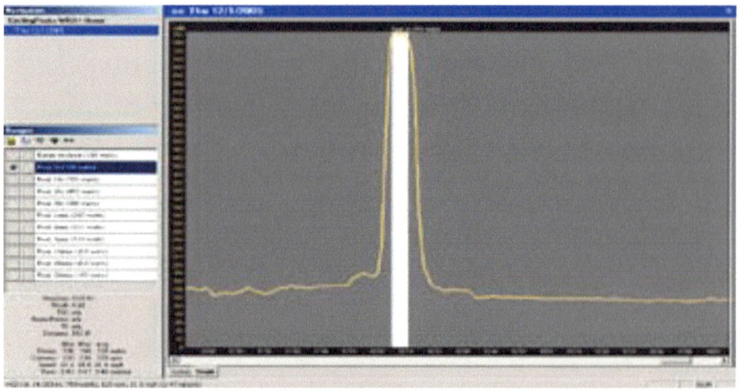

Figure 7-L

So how do we mimic and improve upon this sprint? Let's start by resetting the best fit lines to the parameters we originally created in the .erg file. Click over to the Standard Editing tab and select "Shark Fin". Click "Insert New (After Sel.)", then click the Shape button in the Move Sooner area. Set P1 and P2 at 750, and set T1 as five seconds, T2 as seven seconds, and T3 as 00:01 (steep). Click on the best fit line in the graph that was the *Intellicoach Erg+* interpretation of the workout and click "Delete Selection". The resulting graph should look like Figure 7-N.

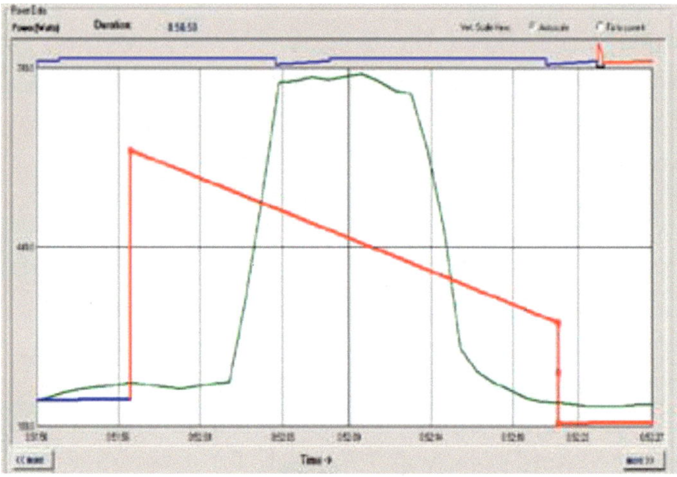

Figure 7-M

Now, let's take the 759 watts we know this rider is capable of for five seconds (the peak five-second average we found in *Cycling Peaks*), and increase it by 5% instead of 3%. Replace the 750 watts in P1 and P2 with 759. Then, click and drag a zoom box around the sprint. Click over to the Scale Workout tab and set the scale factor to 5%. Make sure that "Only Shapes In Current View Range" is selected, and click "OK + Again" once. Click back to the Standard Editing tab – the 759's have become 797's (see Figure 7-O).

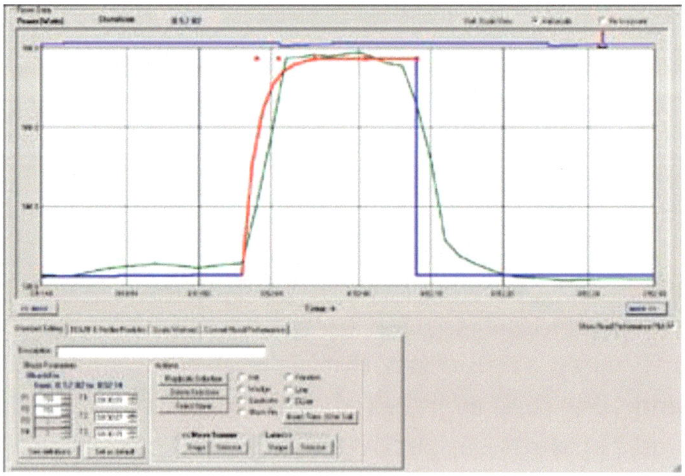

Figure 7-N

The wattage increase isn't terribly much, but it will be exciting to see if my client can continue improving his sprints at this rate. At his body weight, he needs to be capable of 1200-1400 watts over five and 10 seconds to make the hole shot in his Cyclo-Cross events and win some sprint finishes next year. Of course, with good training, the need for a sprint might not be necessary!

Zoom out to see the entire graph. Click over to the Standard Editing tab, select "DLine", make sure that the load line for the sprint is red, and click "Insert New (After Sel.)". Set P1 at 100, P2 at 150, and T1 at five minutes. Then, adjust T1 downward until the overall workout duration reads 57 minutes. The image may be hard to read, but it will look like Figure 7-P.

Save as "2by20at216w797wsprint.erp", and convert to an .erg file. Then, practice taking some of the other .cdf and .txt files you've saved in the past and play with them in the same way.

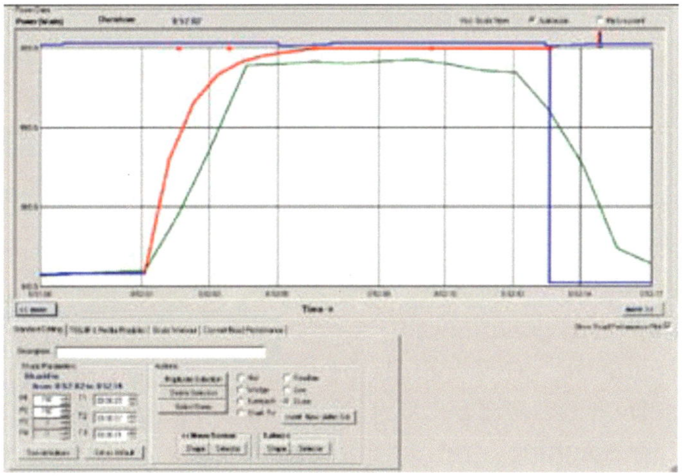

Figure 7-O

NOTES

CyclingPeaks lets you look at things on both a short-term, single-workout basis, and also on a long-term basis, looking for trends and following the Training Stress Scores (TSS), Intensity Factors (IF), and Normalized Power for intervals and overall events.

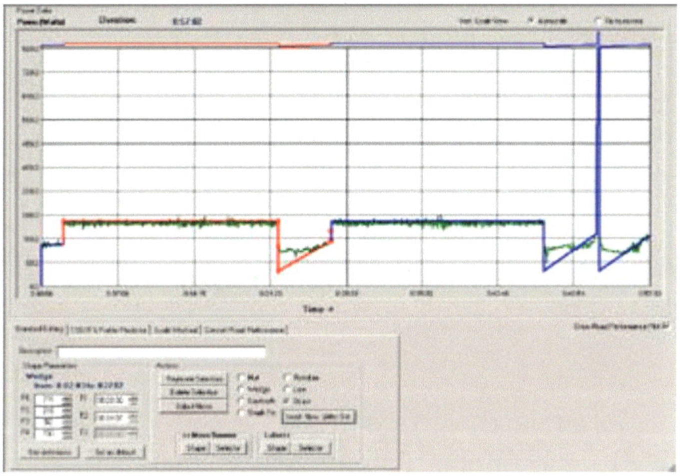

Figure 7-P

Intellicoach Erg+ lets you create and adjust custom workouts and compare your actual performance to what you had planned to do.

Keep in mind that in everything we have just done, we have only been manipulating *one* (intensity) of the three F.I.T. variables. You can also manipulate time (duration) of your workouts, but I believe that the current trend in training is to manipulate only one variable at a time. If you play with too many things at once, you tend to lose track of what you're trying to accomplish.

Finally, remember that *Intellicoach Erg+* can take any file from any download and turn it into a readable .erp file. You can take your mountain bike ride, road ride, track event, even your BMX race, and use *Intellicoach Erg+* to assess how hard the overall event was and what you accomplished within the event, and then scale it on a micro (one event), meso (several events), and macro (the whole season) scale as far out or back as you want.

Chapter 8: THE SCIENCE OF SPINSCAN: ARGUMENTS AND ENLIGHTENMENT

When SpinScan first debuted on CompuTrainers back in the early/mid '90s, many cyclists were intrigued by what it showed (net torque) and how it showed it (bar graphs). Since then, the debate over the usefulness of SpinScan has grown as the number of CompuTrainer users has grown and as academic professionals have learned more about the positive and negative effects torque, muscle activation, and pedal stroke efficiency have on cyclists. There's a ton of anecdotal evidence out there that spinning – rather than stomping or grinding – makes you a faster cyclist, but there have been very few studies to confirm the claims. So the debate continues.

The SpinScan formula divides the average torque placed on the crank by the maximum torque on the crank, and multiplies by 100 (see Figure 8-A).

$$\frac{\bar{T}_{crank}}{T^{max}{}_{crank}} \times 100 = \text{SpinScan}$$

Figure 8-A

Torque and wattage are close cousins – there are ways to get wattage output through high- and low-torque efforts. Torque is also related to cadence, since the pedal stroke is what produces the torque necessary to generate power.

By looking at these values all together on a screen while working out, it may be possible to train your central nervous system to fire the muscles in your legs in a way that produces a more even torque profile, thus minimizing drag and wasted effort. The SpinScan can help teach your legs to work less like pistons – which always have an element of drag in them, particularly in the upstroke – and more like a jet engine turbine. You may have heard the term "pedaling in circles". Theoretically, the SpinScan shows you real-time torque curves so you can see the circles you're pedaling.

I'm not going to discuss the pros and cons of spinning vs. stomping or grinding on the pedals; I'd simply like to urge you to look at your current SpinScan, use it for at least six weeks, and then see if it improves your wattage or speed. My impression is that it *does* work, especially for mountain bikers on steep, sketchy terrain, but the effort involved in re-training the brain can take months or years.

UNDERSTANDING THE SPINSCAN SCREEN

In *CompuTrainer Coaching Software* click “Start”, then select “SpinScan”. Press the F2 key on the CompuTrainer handlebar controller until you see something that looks like the cross-hairs on a rifle scope. The screen will probably be blue or green. Let’s begin by deciphering the screen, so you understand what you’re looking at.

The column on the right displays the following pertinent information:

- Date
- TIME (elapsed time)
- Grade (in percentages; increase/decrease with +/- keys on the handlebar controller)
- DST (distance)
- MPH (current speed)
- AVG MPH (average speed)
- Peak MPH (peak speed)
- Watts (current power)
- Avg Watts (average power)
- Peak Watts (peak power)
- RPM (current cadence)
- Avg RPM (average cadence)
- Peak RPM (peak cadence)
- HR (current heart rate; if you’re using the ear clip or chest-strap converter)
- Avg HR (average heart rate)
- Peak HR (peak heart rate)
- In Zone HR (time spent in the pre-set heart rate range; we won’t use this much)
- PulsePower (see discussion in Chapter 6)
- Weight (body-plus-bike weight)
- Calories (based on kilojoules of energy expenditure; 1 kj ≈ 1.1 Calories)
- RRC (rolling resistance calibration; make sure it’s above 2.5)

Below the big graph area there is some more useful information. In this area, it is important to mentally group items by text color, not necessarily by row or column.

The first row reads:

Left	#	SPINSCAN	#	Right

The number between "Left" and "SPINSCAN" represents the current SpinScan value for your left leg, and the number between "SPINSCAN" and "Right" represents the current SpinScan value for your right leg. These numbers will frequently be different. Notice that the left and right numbers are the same color as the number in the middle of the second row (directly beneath "SpinScan"). These three numbers should be mentally grouped together.

The second row reads:

Avg	#	#	#	Avg

The two outer numbers represent the average SpinScan values over the course of the entire exercise. The middle number is a composite average of the two current SpinScan values (left and right numbers from the first row). Notice that the left and right numbers on the second row are the same color as the number in the middle of the third row. These three numbers should be mentally grouped together.

The third row reads:

L. ATA	#	#	#	R. ATA

ATA (Average Torque Angle) represents the point in each crank's revolution where the highest average torque is being applied. The middle number is a composite average of the two average SpinScan values (left and right numbers from the second row).

The fourth row reads:

%Watts	#		#	%Watts

The two numbers in this row represent the power split between your left and right legs. A normal split range is between 47% and 53%. If one of your legs is much stronger than the other, it will show up here.

It's beyond my scope to explain how RacerMate arrives at these values, and how frequently the values are updated, but it may have something to do with measuring micro-second changes in cadence and torque on a per-stroke basis, as well as wattage fluctuations in the load generator.

Now let's look at the graph itself. The graph is divided into 12 equal pieces, like hours on a clock. Think of your bottom bracket as the center of the clock and your cranks as hour hands, pedaling clockwise around the circle. The numbers around the circle represent the angles of both pedal strokes at once. When your right crank is at the top 0, your left crank is at the bottom 0. Moving clockwise, your cranks pass the 30s at the same time, the 60s, the 90s, and so on.

When you start pedaling, a morphing figure will show up on the graph (see Figure 8-B). This figure shows real-time net torque at positions all over the pedal stroke. The concentric circle in the graph represents the boundary between positive and negative net torque. Most positive torque occurs between the two-o'clock and five-o'clock positions on both cranks (in the two 60-150° ranges on this graph). In a typical pedal stroke, the graph will reflect torque inequality with what I call bulging lobes where there's more positive torque and dips (between the lobes) where there's more negative torque.

All torque is a net of positive and negative torque. You'll always have some drag on your trailing leg; quads and glutes are much stronger than hamstrings and hip flexor muscles. The trick is to modulate your muscle contractions to create more positive torque in your upstroke and save some energy in your downstroke.

The rider in Figure 8-B has a typical pedal stroke, which looks kind of like a Planters' Mr. Peanut silhouette. Most of the positive torque is between the three-o'clock and four-o'clock positions on both legs, indicating that the rider is not actively engaging some muscles in the one-o'clock position at the top of the crank stroke. The dips in the graph indicate a little less hamstring and hip flexor activation in the backstroke and a little less activation of the toe punch muscles when the crank is coming over the top of the stroke. The SpinScan value is in the 50s, the ATA values are in the 100s, and the left/right power split is well balanced at 50% on each side.

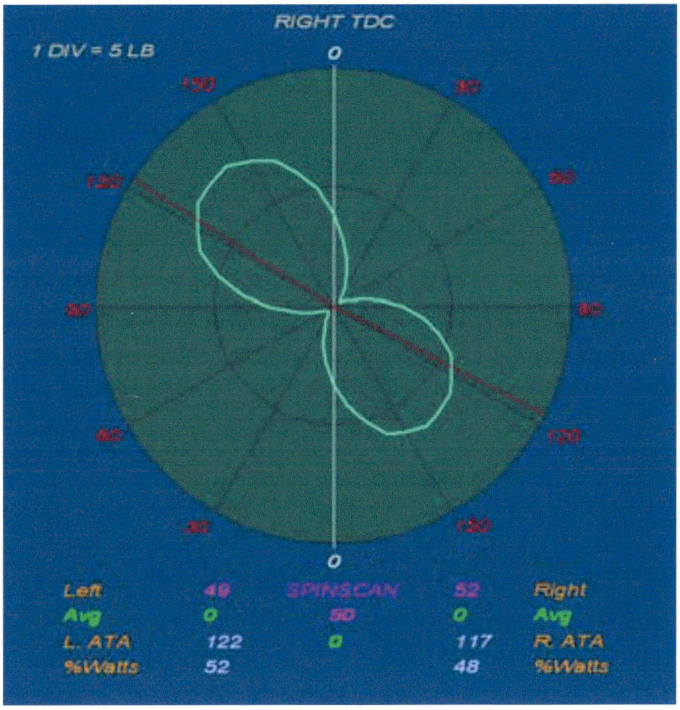

Figure 8-B

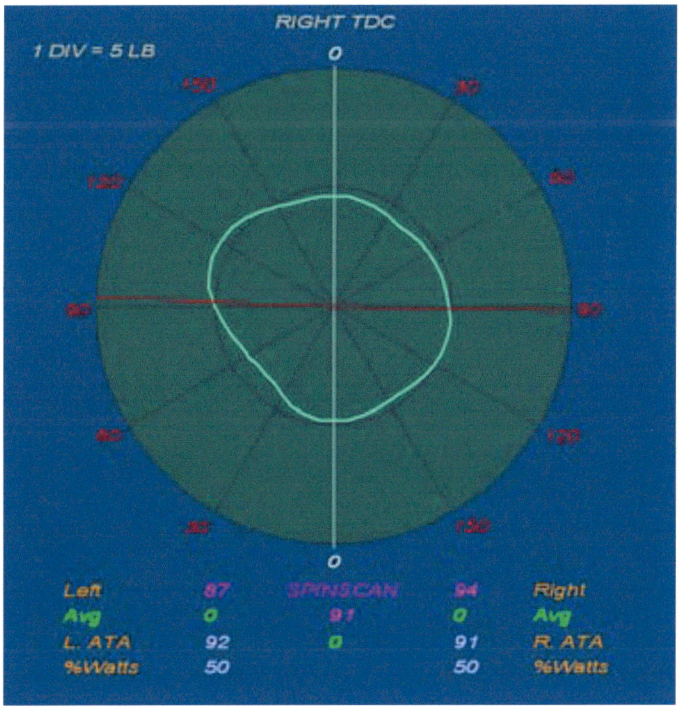

Figure 8-C

Were this rider to spend six weeks working on nothing but his SpinScan — in hopes that he might become a more efficient rider — he might end up with a graph more like the one in Figure 8-C. Notice how much more round it is? It looks more like a chick pea than a peanut. The SpinScan value and the ATA values are in the low 90s, and the left/right power split is still well balanced at 50% on each side. I think this new pedaling profile could possibly lead to more efficient riding.

I'm not going to say for certain that using the SpinScan to learn to pedal in more perfect circles will make you faster — there's just not enough evidence one way or the other. But if you think about it, it does seem to make sense. Applying even pressure against gravity, friction, and axial force — or drag, as it's sometimes called — can help you use the primary movers (quads and glutes) less and the secondary and tertiary movers (hamstrings, hip flexors, anterior tibialis) more, potentially sparing those primary muscles from overuse and fatigue. There are other benefits of steady torque as well. For instance, for mountain bikers, keeping steady torque on a steep, loose incline can sometimes mean the difference between maintaining traction or losing it and having to dismount.

If you're still questioning the validity or benefits of SpinScan, my suggestion is to try it one off-season and see how you feel afterward. No guarantees, but I think you'll be surprised at how much smoother your accelerations and climbs can be.

DOING MORE WITH SPINSCAN

ATA (Average Torque Angle)

Let's do a (mental) experiment here to explain ATA. The ATA value for each leg tells you what angle the crank is at when it's the most effective. The optimal ATA value (the one you want your ATA to read) is the three-o'clock position (90°). Think about it this way: if you placed a five-foot (1.5 m) broomstick a foot away from a wall and let it fall toward the wall, it would hit the wall with very little force. In fact, the broomstick would effectively only be a one-foot (.3 m) lever, and it would only fall through an angle of about 15 degrees.

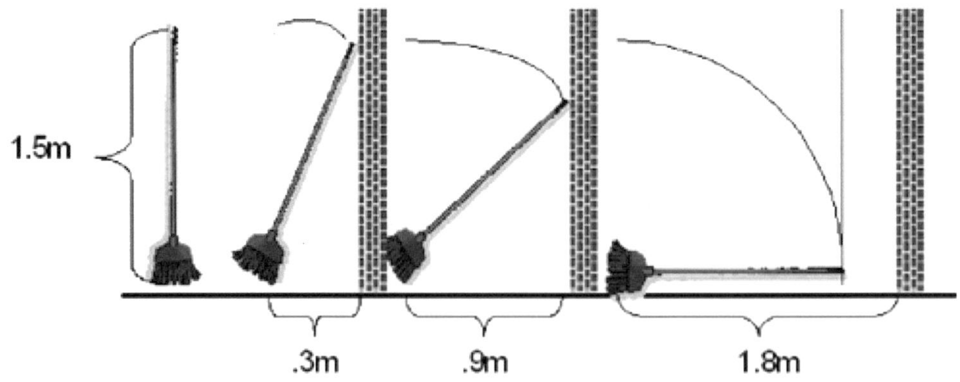

Figure 8-D

If you placed the broomstick three feet (.9 m) away from the wall and let it fall, it might leave a mark on the wall — a result of increased force due to gravity — but it would still only be a three-foot lever. Finally, if you placed the broomstick six feet (1.8 m) away from the wall and let it fall, it would smack onto the floor at maximal speed and force, and you would have the longest lever yet.

A crank is kind of the same — you want the optimal average torque to be the same length or position of the crank length itself, which in most cases is 90 degrees. Going over the 90-degree mark yields an effectively shorter crank again, like when the broomstick was one foot away from the wall, but this time *below* the floor.

When you're riding along on SpinScan, think about whether you would ride faster if you tried to pedal at the very top and bottom of the crank strokes (both 0° marks on the SpinScan) or at some other angle. Play with your pedal stroke and see if you can get your ATA closer to 90. It will probably fatigue the heck out of you at first. I find it helps to think about torque, perpendicular to centrifugal force, which is what's coming out of the cranks. Also, squeezing the pedal inward toward the frame of the bike a bit with my foot seems to help me get a more rounded torque curve, improving my ATA.

Recording SpinScan Sessions

SpinScan sessions can be recorded, saved, and converted into .txt files for *CyclingPeaks* and *Intellicoach Erg+*. The load resistance is based on the *CompuTrainer 3-D* formula, not the *CompuTrainer Coaching Software* .erg formula. Just do your typical warmup, calibrate the device, plug the stereo jack in, and click the F1 button on the handlebar controller. The SpinScan clock will start running, and you'll be able to increase or decrease the wattage load (based on incline) with the + and - keys on the handlebar controller. When you're done, press "RESET" on the handlebar controller, and you will be asked if you want to save the file. Press "F1" (yes), and a Windows Explorer dialog box will open. Older SpinScan workouts used to be saved as .ss files, but with the latest version of *CompuTrainer Coaching Software* you can save the file as a .cdf and convert it to .txt format.

CONCLUSION

SpinScan is all about optimizing your pedal stroke, and there are many ways to do so. Are you trying out a new position? Do five straight days of 30-minute efforts on the SpinScan and save them before moving to the new position. Then do the same *after* the change. Can you identify any trends? Are you truly faster and more efficient in the new posture? What if your SpinScan shows that you're favoring one leg over the other? Mess with your cleat position — and maybe your crank length — and compare.

I won't argue the scientific merits or shortcomings of SpinScan, but I do think that you can improve your performance by using it to record and analyze data. The CompuTrainer and all its software can make it easy to give yourself analysis paralysis, but on the other hand, collecting data for analysis can actually give purpose to every ride. Knowing that you can save and track trends in the data can give you even more confidence that you're improving.

Chapter 9: THE RUBBER HITS THE ROAD: USING THE TESTS AND INTELLICOACH TOOLS

Coach Paul Smeulders (creator of Intellicoach Erg+*) contributed this chapter, in which he relates his experiences using his software on the road and after races to help athletes understand their performances.*

I'm not one to waste time with computers. I always favor really fast, obvious methods whereby I can impart the necessary information to the athlete. Thus, *Intellicoach Erg+* has evolved features that allow me — and *you* — to do just that.

If you haven't noticed by now, one real value of *Intellicoach Erg+* is that it lets you define a training strategy, execute that strategy, and analyze the data from your execution of the strategy, always in the context of that original strategy. So let's take a look at how all that is done with on-road sessions and real-life races.

INTERVAL SESSIONS ANALYSIS

Having read through this book, you can readily appreciate that *Intellicoach Erg+* will find the important aspects of interval sessions. Using *Computrainer Coaching Software* with *Intellicoach Erg+* pretty much guarantees that your interval session will go according to plan. But out on the road, it's a great deal more difficult. Even with a power meter, the urge to overdo it is very high, the terrain is not always amenable to the plan, and you may find that following your plan is very difficult.

First, you need to find terrain that suits your session. For regular intervals, find a flat course so you can control your power and so you won't be forced to recover on ascents or do efforts on descents. A flat Criterium loop without sharp corners is really good for this. For hill intervals, find a *single* hill that you can repeat with adequate rest between, rather than a succession of irregularly spaced hills that force your recovery and effort times to be unsuitable. This doesn't mean you can't do unstructured or downhill intervals some days, it just means that you will have more success in meeting the goals of your session if — just as you did indoors with *Intellicoach Erg+* — you do a little planning beforehand.

Figure 9-A shows a power trace from an intervals session done on the road with a Power-Tap, and analyzed using *Intellicoach Erg+*. After downloading the Power-Tap, the user adjusted the intervals-fitting sliders to line up reasonably with the data. (You can use the upper two sliders to adjust the sensitivity of the fit, and then use the lower slider to knock out some of the tiny little intervals that a sensitive fit would show, but which may be uninteresting to you.)

This athlete refused to believe his testing results could predict his intervals capability. He did his first intervals way too hard, as shown by the extreme downward slope of the initial intervals. A little downward slope is usually there, but clearly this rider needed to reduce his interval power as the workout progressed. He was over-reaching.

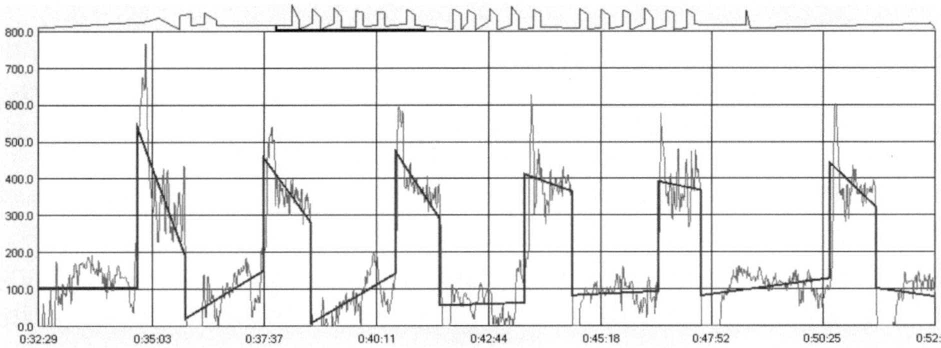

Figure 9-A

On the other hand, the session represented in Figure 9-B was a very well-executed session. The coach, in trying to find improvement points, instructed this athlete to rest a little bit more between efforts, as she clearly ramped up her power while resting in anticipation of her interval. This may have detracted from the power she could have produced in the effort time.

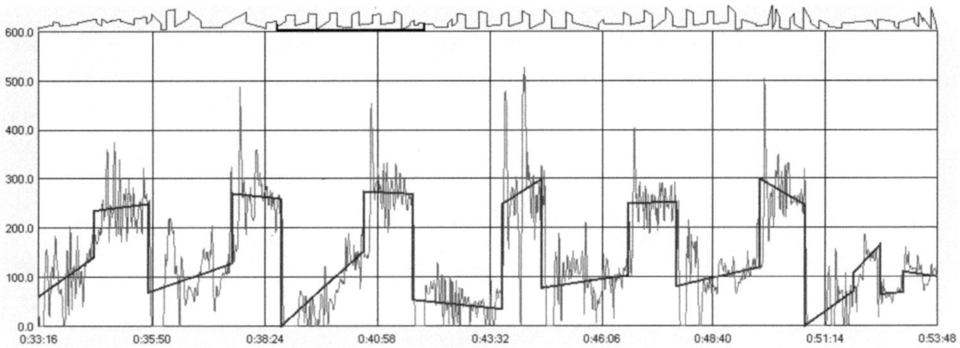

Figure 9-B

When you're looking at your own workout files, switch from Wedges to Hats to get the average power of each interval and rest, as well as the timing of each interval. These can be exported in a report that you can open in Excel. Click "File", then "Save Intervals/Mapping Summary to .csv" from the main window's menu. Of course, you can save the file to be repeated, scaled, or executed again later on your CompuTrainer.

TIME TRIAL PREDICTION AND POST-TIME-TRIAL ANALYSIS

There are many theories behind what constitutes a good time trial. It is not my goal here to push any one particular viewpoint. What I will do is show how the *Intellicoach Erg+* analyzer can be used to quickly view a time trial performance, and discuss only one of the prevailing theories.

The theory is as follows: A flat 15km time trial is largely an aerobic event, but will be done above your one-hour threshold — more likely at your 20-25 minute critical power, which by now you should have measured and taken the time to understand.

Going deeply anaerobic too soon or too often will force a recovery phase after each trip to the land of anaerobia. Frequent small excursions into an anaerobic state tends to reduce overall average power and time, due to the recovery required. Similarly, less frequent but very deep excursions into the anaerobic zone may have the same effect.

The goal is to approach and steadily sustain the power level that one can sustain for the expected critical time, and if there is anything left near the end, *then* risk anaerobia just at the end of the race, when you know you can sustain the anaerobic power level for the remaining time. Some people set out below the target level, and as the race progresses, ratchet the power up toward the target, perhaps at every quarter of the race distance, or just increase the power after the halfway point. This is a great way to prevent overdoing the first part of the race.

Let's make this our strategy, and state it this way: "My average power should remain at or below my 20-minute power on the outbound leg. After the turn, I'll increase it by 10 watts if I can, and about 1.5-2 minutes (1-1.5 km) from the finish, I'll crush it, and ride steadily at my five-minute max power, or more if I've got it closer to the end." (We use the five-minute and not the two-minute power due to the fatigue you'll already have thanks to the initial part of the race.

Don't fret too much if you are a 25-minute 15 km rider. Just examine a recent *Intellicoach Profiler* curve estimate for 25 minutes, and make that the power you want to target. Add five watts or so to account for the enthusiasm for the race, and to bring yourself to a better game.

Now go out and try that, and come back to *Intellicoach Erg+* after the race. Record *all* of your race data, including your warmup, so you can gain some insights. Import your road performance just as described before, but import the file from your on-road power meter. *Intellicoach Erg+* will directly convert Polar files and Power-Tap files. SRM and Ergomo files need to be exported to SRM text using the software supplied by those manufacturers, or using *CyclingPeaks*. Instructions are in the *Intellicoach Erg+* help files. The default Wedge fit analyzer will do the fitting, and you will immediately get a sense of whether your race was steady or not. Your trace might look like the one in Figure 9-C.

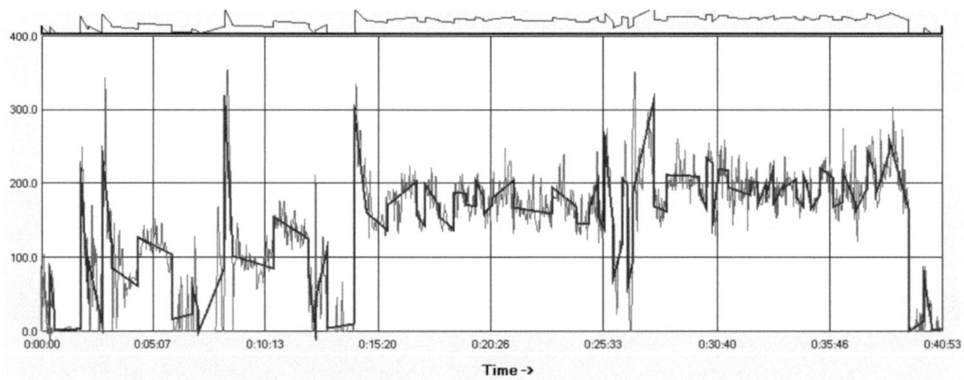

Figure 9-C

We'll skip analyzing the warmup and go straight to the race itself. It is clear from the power trace where the race begins. It's the big increase just before the long steady effort in power. You could use the intervals analyzer for this (as shown in Figure 9-C), but you might get more intervals than you care for, especially at the turnaround point, or if the effort was not very steady.

It appears this rider didn't do a good job of holding steady power. However, it was recorded from a power meter which she had covered up (since we wanted to see how she normally rides time trials). It shows a great deal of undulations. This course also has a highway overpass just before the turnaround. But we want to analyze in the context of our strategy and goal, which in this case was steady power output, increasing in the second half, with an anaerobic burst at the end.

Click on the Marker Mode button. The display will show a blue line which is the average power of the whole green trace. It isn't important at all, especially if your warmup is shown in the data. You will also see Average and Trend buttons. For now, leave it on Average. It also has instructions to use Shift + right click to set time markers sequentially at points of interest. So let's try that.

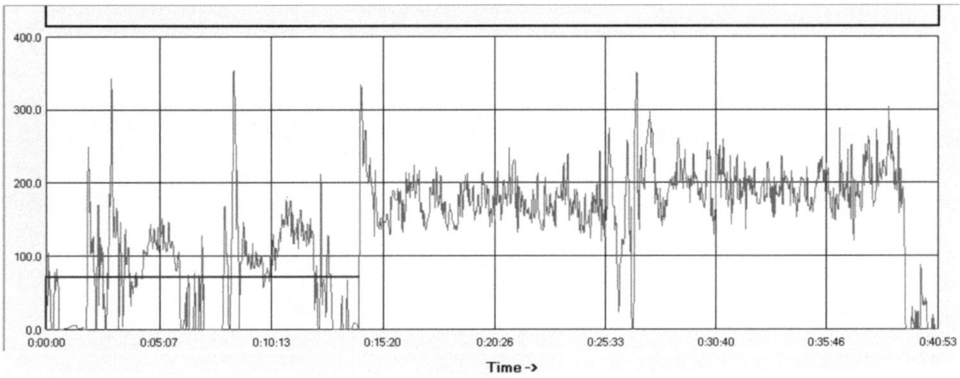

Figure 9-D

Point your mouse anywhere on the graph, such as the time where the race starts. While holding down the Shift key, click the right button on your mouse. The line becomes shorter, and moves to the average power level of the workout up to that point (see Figure 9-D). This is the average power for your warmup, and it is unimportant. There should have been some intervals there, for which you can use the intervals analyzer later, on your own.

Point the mouse to where you think you turned around (shown by a vast reduction in power near the halfway time). Shift + right click, and you'll see a new line appear showing the average power between the first marker you made and this new marker (the outbound leg of your race). Shift + right click again while pointing to the time where you believe you started your final crush. And finally, Shift + right click at your finish. If you don't like where you placed a marker, just back up the cursor to before that point, and click again, or click "Intervals Fit" and then "Marker Fit" to reset the markers completely.

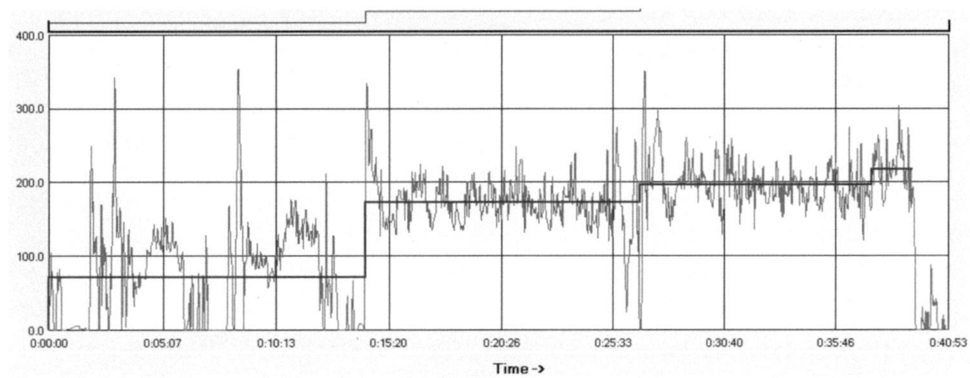

Figure 9-E

Now you should have a set of lines that represent your average power levels during the three planned phases of your time trial (see Figure 9-E). Click on the first line of your time trial powers — it will turn red — and then go to the Standard Editing tab. Your average power will show up in the P1 box, and your outbound split time to the turn around will be in the T1 box. Click to highlight the next line you marked, and you will see the average power of the return leg up to the crush. Finally, click on the line representing your final effort, and look at those powers.

You can save a file that can be read by Excel. Click “File”, then “Save Intervals/Mapping Summary to .csv” from the main window’s menu. For the rider in the example, the averages are 174 on the outbound, 197 on the return, and 218 on the final crush. Not bad for not watching the power meter. But if she had been able to watch the meter, she probably would have ridden steadier overall, and a little harder on the outbound leg.

Now here’s the cool part. With the race showing in the display, and with all of your markers visible, go to the Convert Road Performance tab and click “Trend” in the Marker Mode box. Now you can see clearly if your power was decreasing or increasing throughout your race phases. Figure 9-F shows this capability, with the workout of a rider who had a non-constant tendency.

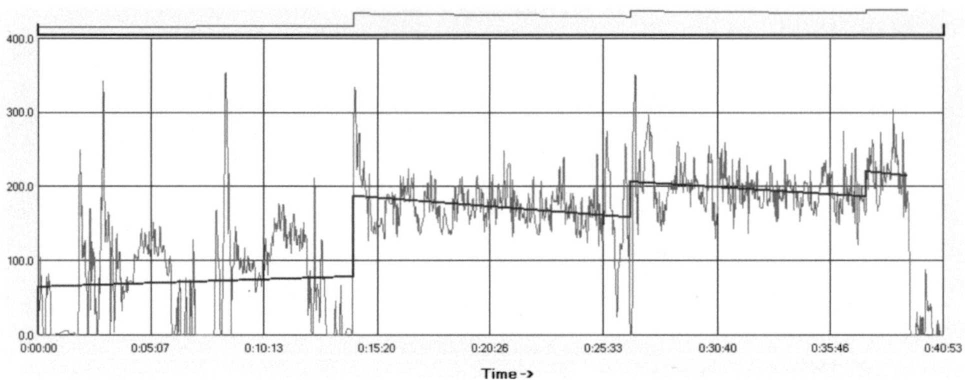

Figure 9-F

She is struggling hard to maintain a pacing strategy, and some of this is likely from her periodic overpower efforts we saw as a series of detected intervals. Although she succeeded in increasing her power on the return leg, it was still a steady decrease. It must be said that the downhill section toward the turn on this course always causes the outbound leg to look worse than it really was, and relocating markers may be a good exercise, as shown in Figure 9-G. This is actually very good for someone riding blind to their power output.

Now you can view your race in the context of your intent. You can criticize your own strategy, tune it, and commit to better execution next time.

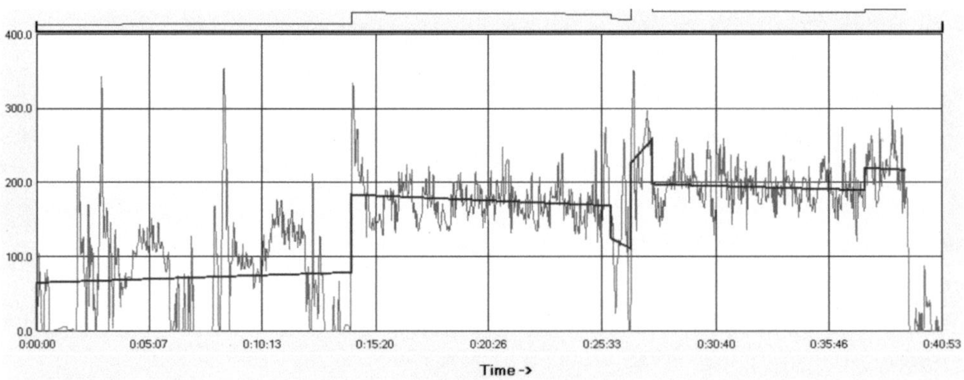

Figure 9-G

For good measure, let's look at a really well-executed time trial (see Figure 9-H). This guy could see his meter, and rode 394 watts outbound, 398 watts inbound, and 479 watts in the final minute. The overpass and downhill to the turnaround is very clear, as is the same overpass on the return leg.

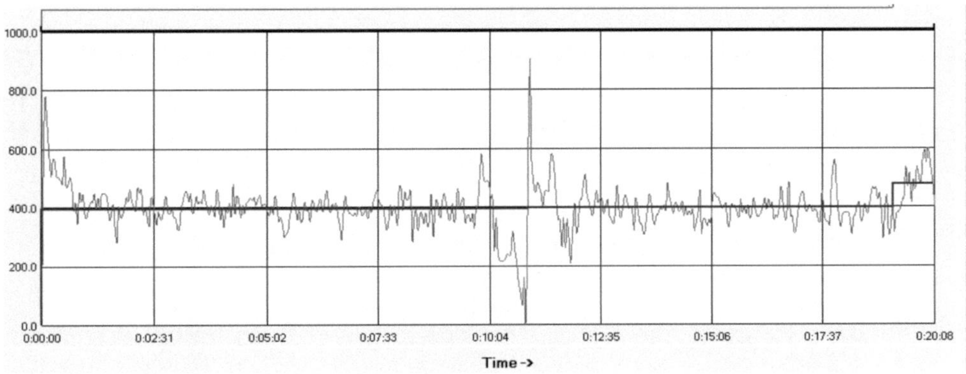

Figure 9-H

I'm not saying that this is the best way for *you* to ride a time trial. However, this method of analysis is probably the best way to assess the performance goal that you set prior to the race. There are a couple of ways to improve:

- Stick to the strategy for a few more time trials, and improve your execution of the strategy, as revealed by *Intellicoach Erg+*.
- Change the strategy altogether, and learn to execute your new strategy, hopefully resulting in improved times. If not, change strategy again.
- Forget all about strategy for now, go set a blistering time, post-analyze your race, and adopt whatever "pops out" as your subsequent strategy. I highly doubt that this option will actually result in a lifetime personal best, but that possibility is always open with *IntelliCoach Erg+*.

Finally, you can train with your Marker Mode workout on your CompuTrainer, just as you could all other workouts in the manual. Go ahead and scale up the power as you improve, and determine what you can handle for your next competition!

Chapter 10: PSYCHOLOGICAL SKILLS FOR CYCLISTS: BUILDING A ROADMAP TO THE ZONE

Here, Dr. Robert S. Neff graciously allows me to include Chapter 1 of his book entitled Entering the Zone. *This chapter will help you overcome mental and physical obstacles during those times when you aren't accomplishing your goals.*

"If one does not know to which port he is sailing, no wind is favorable."
— Seneca

CREATING THE ROADMAP

Before beginning any journey, it's critical that you know where you want to go, why you want to go there, what roadblocks will likely get in your way, and how you will try to solve those problems if you encounter them. Let's imagine you want to drive to Canada for a vacation. If you've made the trip before, or have someone with you who has, it's a huge advantage. If not, a company like AAA can create a detailed map showing exactly where to go and even when to detour to avoid construction and traffic. You can easily look ahead and make plans to avoid problem areas.

After you finish the worksheets in this chapter, you will have constructed a roadmap to your highest dreams. You will know where you are going and what you will have to do along the way. This will be your first draft, which will get more detailed with experience and by applying what you learn from others who have gone before you. Read biographies of greats in your sport. Find experienced coaches who have gone where you are headed or have helped others to get there. As you gain this knowledge of what difficulties to expect during your journey, you'll be able to create solutions long before problems ever happen. Even if you can't avoid a problem, you'll have a plan to get you through it. The following sections will provide solutions to common mental roadblocks encountered by athletes with high goals.

One of the most important factors that drive people to be successful is their "why". Why are they doing what they're doing? Why did Michael Jordan, for example, work so hard at his basketball skills even after people acknowledged him as one of the best players in the game? Why was he always the first to practice and the last to leave? Why did he continue doing his weights on game days and even during the playoffs? Was it because he was trying to prove something to his high school coach who cut him from the team? Was it because he wanted an NBA championship ring? Three rings in a row? Was it because he wanted to be known as the best player of all-time? Whatever it is, Jordan and every other great athlete have strong reasons WHY they compete.

The Bigger the Why

When you have a big enough "why", the "how" becomes easy. Talk show host Oprah Winfrey once interviewed a man who had a big "why". His daughter was dying and needed a kidney transplant. He wanted to donate one of his, but he was obese and the doctors refused. They said he had to lose 100 pounds in eight months. He had been trying for years to lose weight but couldn't do it. He was in good company — there are millions of people who can't seem to lose any weight. But this man did it — and with a month to spare. He said it was easy because he had such an important reason why — to save his daughter. As soon as his "why" was big enough, the "how" became clear, and even easy.

Here are some "why" examples from successful athletes: to prove it to themselves or others; they enjoy achieving; they enjoy improving; they want praise, admiration, or approval; to be more attractive to others; to take care of others; to give thanks; to show respect to God for giving them skills; to leave a legacy; to make the world a better place; to be happy; to feel good about themselves; to have more time; to have more money; to get healthier; to improve a life; to save a life. Why will you go through all the sacrifice and pain to be successful?

Exercise A: List your five biggest cycling-related dreams and your "why" for each.

	DREAMS	WHY
1		
2		
3		
4		
5		

Additional forms can be found at www.roadmaptothezone.com.

Exercise B: For each dream, list the biggest potential roadblocks, and the best solutions.

	ROADBLOCKS	SOLUTIONS
1	a)	
	b)	
	c)	
2	a)	
	b)	
	c)	
3	a)	
	b)	
	c)	
4	a)	
	b)	
	c)	
5	a)	
	b)	
	c)	

Additional forms can be found at www.roadmaptothezone.com.

Exercise C: Create a Roadmap to your highest dream.

Here's an example of what you're about to create using the goals you've just written in Exercise A and B. These are the goals of a young cyclist regarding his ideal career. Notice they are chronological (ordered by date) and progressive (listed from the present to the future, starting at the bottom), but they are not completely controllable by him. That's okay at this point – he will later create a list of controllable actions for each goal as he progresses up the Roadmap.

Category: Cycling Career

ROADMAP	
GOAL	**TARGET DATE**
Qualify for USA Olympic Team	Sept, 2012
↑ Qualify for US National Team	June, 2009
↑ Qualify for Category 2	May, 2007
↑ Qualify for Category 3	June, 2005
↑ Qualify for Category 4	April, 2004 – DONE!

Today's Date:___/___/___

Update by:___/___/___ (every 180 days)

Additional forms can be found at www.roadmaptothezone.com.

Directions for Creating Your Roadmap:

1. Draw the form from the next page on a blank piece of paper (or, you can download it from www.roadmaptothezone.com).
2. Write your biggest sport-related dream (from Exercise A). We're asking you to start with the end in mind, so make sure this dream is the final major accomplishment you hope to achieve.
3. Put a box around it.
4. Draw a short arrow pointing up at the bottom of the box you just made.
5. Work down the page, writing the most significant accomplishment you will need to achieve in order to reach the higher box.
6. Continue until you get to present day (this lowest goal should be your next major accomplishment).
7. Now go back up the page, writing a target date for each goal in the right column.
8. Write in today's date, and the date 60 days from now when you will update this goal sheet.
9. Compare your Roadmap to the sample on the previous page. They should look similar.
10. Post your Roadmap in a visible place (bathroom mirror, on the wall, in your locker, etc.). You want to see this sheet every day!

ROADMAP	
GOAL	TARGET DATE

Today's Date: ___/___/___

Update by: ___/___/___ (every 60 days)

Additional forms can be found at www.roadmaptothezone.com.

"A goal is a dream with a deadline."
— Napoleon Hill

Exercise D: Using the Roadmap you just created, make a list of five key things you have to do to reach the next goal on your sheet.

This list should include controllable things only. This is your action list. For example, if a cyclist's next major goal is to qualify for the nationals, the action list might include things like improving fitness, improving a technical weakness, studying performance videos, reducing negative self-talk, scheduling tougher practice rides, etc. Be specific about what you will do each week and by when.

Next Major Goal: ______________________________

FIVE KEY THINGS TO MOVE ME TO THIS GOAL	
1	
2	
3	
4	
5	

NOTE: See the *Single-Step Motivational Software* description at the end of this chapter. You can download a free trial and use it to track the goals you just created.

VISUALIZATION: SEEING IT BEFORE YOU BELIEVE IT

You know the old saying, "I'll believe it when I see it"? If you've ever said that to yourself, you probably meant that you didn't believe something was ever going to happen and that you'd need to see it first. Unfortunately, high performance doesn't quite work that way. In fact, anybody who ever achieved anything of significance saw it in their mind first (imagined it), and then believed it was possible to bring into reality. Examples include: Bannister breaking the four-minute mile; Armstrong landing on the moon; Bell inventing the telephone; and the Wright Brothers succeeding at manned flight. In every case, these people clearly saw in their minds that it was possible before anyone else believed it. They had a mental picture of what they were going to do long before they actually did it. Imagining it enhanced their belief that it was possible to do. This process of creating an ideal image in your mind to improve the chances of it actually happening is called visualization.

What is Visualization (or Visual Imagery)?

It's a picture in your mind – like a movie – on the movie screen of your mind. You have control over what you want to put on the screen. It is something that should be done along with physical practice (you can't perform consistently well without actually going out and practicing), but you also need to visualize clearly in order to perform well. Visual imagery practiced consistently will help you to physically perform what you're visualizing better.

Why Would I Practice Visualizing?

The first reason is to learn skills or sequences that occur in competition (visualizing strengthens the neural pathways – your nerves fire almost exactly the same as if you were really physically doing the activity). Next, you might visualize to practice skills or sequences you've recently learned. Visualization also can be used to control nervousness (the more times you see the ideal happening, the more confident you will feel – also, practicing remaining calm makes it more likely you'll make that choice when you feel stress). Finally, athletes often use visualization to help remember skills or sequences during periods of injury (visualizing makes it easier to perform after healing).

How Do I Visualize?

Visualization is much clearer and more controllable when you are calm (no tightness, anger or nervousness). To help you learn to control your muscle tension, it's good to practice a relaxation sequence that teaches your body to relax whenever you need (see Appendix A and B [of Dr. Neff's book, *Entering the Zone*]). Some people struggle with visualizing, but everyone can do it. Try visualizing as you read the paragraph below. Be sure to visualize looking out of your own eyes (first person) instead of as an observer watching yourself. First-person visualizing allows the images to be very similar to what you'd actually see if you were doing it, and, it enables you to actually *feel* what it's like (kinesthetic response). Read the next paragraph and visualize doing what it describes.

"You are in your bedroom, sitting on your bed. Stand up and walk over to the door. Reach out and open the door. Notice which hand you used. See the type of handle on the door and imagine feeling the breeze created by the door passing in front of your face. Go through the door and walk to the kitchen. See what is on the walls as you go. Imagine you are barefoot, and feel the floor surface(s) as you walk. Turn on the kitchen light and walk over to the fridge. Open the door and see that the fridge is empty except for a jar of dill pickles. You are hungry and thirsty. Take the jar out and feel how heavy and cold the jar is. Twist off the top and hear it pop open. Take a pickle out. It's cold and slimy. Take a big bite. Hear the crunch and taste the pickle. Now pick up the jar with both hands and take a big drink of the cold pickle juice."

Most people have never done this, but you probably imagined doing it just fine! The point is, even if (for example) you've never performed well in front of a large audience, you *can* imagine doing so. Visualizing being successful will make it easier for you to actually perform successfully in front of large audiences.

Visualization Practice Ideas

Use the descriptions below to improve the quality of your mental images. It should be easiest to imagine familiar objects and short trips you take often. Visualizing far away or imaginary locations can be more challenging if you've never visited them. Many people imagine beautiful locations while they try to calm themselves down. Lastly, visualize performing your sport or activity. Because of the changing nature of sport, it is easier to tape record sequences that are most likely to happen and then visualize them being done successfully. However, many athletes imagine themselves performing well in front of large crowds and dealing with all the adversity that would occur. This helps them to feel more comfortable when they are actually in that competitive situation.

1 **Objects:** Visualize these items to increase your control over images. Directions: look at the object, then close your eyes and try to see the shape and color clearly.

a) your shoes
b) your newest bike
c) your toothpaste container
d) your car
e) any other object that seems interesting

2 **Trips:** Visualize to improve your ability to see details. Directions: Imagine yourself going somewhere and pay attention to what is there (things, colors, and smells).

a) the walk from your bedroom to your kitchen
b) the ride from home to work or school
c) a walk around the outside of your house
d) one lap around the track (actually time yourself!)
e) imagine anything involving you moving somewhere

3 **Locations:** These are usually used to relax or motivate. Directions: Imagine yourself being somewhere and then try to actually make your body experience it (scenery, temperature, sounds, and smells).

a) lying on a warm sandy beach with a cool ocean breeze
b) sitting in the middle of an open field full of flowers
c) sitting in an outside hot tub with snow falling all around you
d) riding through a valley surrounded by enormous mountains
e) any place that might relax you

4 **Performance:** Cyclists routinely practice visualizing performances to increase success during competition. Directions: Imagine a situation that you want to improve and then make it go well for you (if it starts to go bad, say, "STOP!", rewind your mental tape, and play it through again until you see yourself do it properly).

a) **Before an Important Race:** Work at imagining the scenery in as much detail as possible. See your other competitors, feel your bike, be aware of the weather. Imagine yourself in the ideal performance state: calm, intense, focused, confident. The gun goes off and you accelerate fast, immediately passing through the middle pack to within shooting distance of the front.

b) **During a Race:** You are going to lead a breakaway. It's a strategy you've been planning for weeks. You know the course well, and you know exactly where you're aiming to do it. If the situation changes such that it is no longer a smart move tactically, you'll pass on it. As you ride within 50 yards of your breakaway area, there is an accident ahead. You decide to make your move now. Your adrenalin pumps through your veins and you surge away. It was the ideal distraction for a breakaway.

c) **Toward the End of a Race:** You have been toward the front of the breakaway pack, or leading, for most of the race. As you enter the final 400 yards you feel strong and powerful. Your breathing is deep and clear, and you are ready for anything. A group of three riders makes a break. You react quickly and follow in behind. With 100 yards, you pull to the outside and explode past the group. Your exceptional fitness and technique keeps you there as you cross the finish line.

Exercise E: List the five most common sequences or actions that occur in competitive cycling. Examples might include: drafting, breaking away, changing a tire, etc.

	FIVE MOST COMMON SEQUENCES OR ACTIONS THAT OCCUR IN COMPETITIVE CYCLING
1	
2	
3	
4	
5	

Exercise F: List three sequences or actions you need to improve most — or that you need to execute well — to win.

	THREE SEQUENCES OR ACTIONS I NEED TO IMPROVE MOST — OR EXECUTE WELL — TO WIN
1	
2	
3	

"The greatest mistake you can make in life is to be continually thinking you will make one."
— Proverb

SELF-TALK TRAINING

One of the most frustrating things performers must deal with is negative self-talk. Imagine you are at an important competition. You have only a few minutes before you're on. Then it occurs to you, "What if I mess up? What if I perform badly and lose? What if..." Suddenly you get so nervous you have trouble breathing. These kinds of self-doubts contribute to stage fright, choking, and under-performance. The good news is, we can learn to change and even block the harmful self-talk that leads to nervousness and fear.

You Are What You Say You Are

Everyone thinks negative thoughts at times. Only when people learn to recognize negative thoughts, stop them, and replace them with positives will they be able to consistently perform well. If you tell yourself enough times that you are no good, you'll start believing it. Self-fulfilling prophecies are commonplace. Similarly, if you tell yourself you are a talented athlete, you will eventually believe this as well. Unfortunately, most athletes aren't even aware of the thoughts they think during competition.

Thought Control Sequence

Use the following sequence to stop negative or self-destructive thoughts:

First, RECOGNIZE the negative thought.
Say "STOP", "MAYBE", or "WHATEVER".
Then REPLACE the negative thought with a positive word.
Finally, think STRATEGY.

The following three tables list common thoughts athletes have during competition. Use the first list to help you recognize the negative thoughts you have, and then the next two lists as ideas with which to replace the negative thoughts.

Negatives After a Mistake

The following is a list of negative thoughts after mistakes. This list is provided because most athletes don't realize they have negative self-talk. Before anything can be done to improve self-talk, you must first recognize the negative. Feel free to add your thoughts!

I suck!	Ahhhhhhhh!	No Way!	Choker!
Any four-letter word	Loser!	That was weak!	Come oooooon!
I quit!	I'm so bad!	I'm the worst!	You idiot!
I stink!	You're no athlete!	I'm pitiful!	How could I miss?
Why me?	Any sarcasm	What was that?	Just don't miss!
That was so easy!	I hate this sport!	Merry Christmas!	Oh, that's just great!

Positives After a Mistake

This list of positives is the most important list. Athletes can't always prevent errors from happening. All they can do is manage the mistake well, put it behind them, and move on with an optimistic outlook.

Next point.	Take your time.	Keep fighting!
Forget it.	Calm down.	High percentage.
One at a time.	Stay tough!	Good effort.

Other Helpful Words

This list is a series of shorter cue words you might use to replace negative thoughts.

Relax	React	Present
Focus	Quick	Fight
Control	Positive	Breathe

Thought Control Exercises

Gap Thinking

This is a simple exercise to begin, but not an easy one to maintain. Close your eyes and become aware of your thoughts. Now become aware of the gaps between your thoughts. Try to stay in the gap between thoughts. When a thought comes in, simply recognize its existence and then get back into the gap. The length of time you stay in the gap is not as important as staying present to the thoughts that come into your mind and then re-focusing back into the gap.

Past/Present/Future Labeling

Write down thoughts you remember having before, during, or after a competition. Now label them as past, present, or future (Example of a past thought: "I can't believe I just made that mistake!"). Notice how negative emotions (anger, nervousness) are tied to thoughts that exist in the past or future. Positive emotions (love, happiness, confidence) are often present thoughts. Choose present thoughts during competition.

Rational/Irrational Labeling

Write down thoughts you remember having before, during, or after a competition. Label them as rational (make sense) or irrational (make no sense). For example: "I always make that mistake!" That would be irrational because you don't *always* make that mistake. Work at rewording your thoughts so they are rational and accurate ("I make that mistake when I get rushed. Be patient.").

Perception/Reality Labeling

This exercise involves you observing events in your world and describing them. Your goal is to describe only what actually happened, not your perception of the event. For example, when describing a touchdown, your perception might be, "The quarterback threw the pass too hard, and I was lucky to hang on to it." But what *actually happened* was, "The quarterback threw a pass and I caught it for a touchdown." Notice how stating just the facts can reduce emotion surrounding an event.

Other Labeling

Helpful/Harmful (just recognizing how helpful or harmful a thought is can help); Permanent/Temporary (great athletes describe problems as temporary and successes as permanent); Lucky/Skillful (attributing success to luck is usually only done so one appears humble — great athletes consistently relate success to skill since it is more of a permanent factor); Controllable/Uncontrollable (successful athletes focus on factors they control — to do otherwise leads to feelings of helplessness and stress).

A Description of Ideal Thoughts

Before Competition

Thoughts should be in the present or slight future, focusing on the ideal strategy. You should be sure to remain rational, keeping thoughts simple and unemotional. Stay in reality, on things you know to be true. All thoughts should be helpful and supportive. If you can't control it, don't worry about it.

During Competition

Work at staying in the gap as much as possible. It's safe there, since there are no thoughts to distract you or cause unwanted emotion. Perform on automatic as much as possible. If you have thoughts, keep them in the present, helpful, and related to effort and strategy, both controllable by you.

After Competition

To learn from what happened, you obviously need to get into the past and evaluate your performance. Be constructive when criticizing and be sure to make a list of controllable suggestions so you can take action on them immediately.

Exercise G: Write down thoughts you remember having before, during or after a recent competition.

List as many as you can remember, each on a separate line. Label each thought as: Past, Present, or Future; Rational or Irrational; Perception or Reality; Helpful or Harmful; and Temporary or Permanent.

Here's an example: "If I try to break away, no one ever follows." Answer: Future, Irrational, Perception, Harmful, Permanent.

RECENT THOUGHTS DURING COMPETITION					
THOUGHT	PAST PRESENT FUTURE	RATIONAL IRRATIONAL	PERCEPTION REALITY	HELPFUL HARMFUL	TEMPORARY PERMANENT

Additional forms are available at www.roadmaptothezone.com.

"The degree of one's emotions varies inversely with one's ability to think clearly."
— Bertrand Russell

PUTTING IT ALL TOGETHER

To summarize what's been covered in this chapter so far, you know where you want to go, you know how you'll get there, you have a plan for overcoming adversity, you can imagine yourself succeeding, and your self-talk is helping you. This section is about how to actually find the zone once the competition starts.

When athletes of all sports are "in the zone," they report feeling unbelievably confident about their ability to perform well. Even after mistakes, athletes feel as though they can bounce back with a high level of performance. Many report feeling excited, like children before opening presents. They can hardly wait to compete — to see what terrific combination of things they'll put together next. Athletes who are zoning often find themselves smiling — regardless of how well they are doing — because they are enjoying themselves so much. Pro golfer Phil Mickelson demonstrated this perfectly as he smiled his way to a 2004 Masters win.

When describing how they feel, athletes often use words like carefree, effortless, automatic, powerful, energized, and simple. The following is a newspaper quote from a tennis player who had just won a tournament in California:

"I wish I could control what just happened. I had confidence that I've never felt before — I really believed I could do ANYTHING! This is what it's all about — this is why I play tennis — not just to win tournaments — but to feel the way I did out there today. If I could feel that way more often, I'd be the best in the world." This quote came from Pete Sampras, before he turned pro. Sampras went on to win more Grand Slams than any other man. Perhaps he learned to control that feeling that leads to the zone!

How to Increase the Chances of Zoning

Before the Competition

1 **Learn and Practice Efficient Technique:** Efficient movements have less tendency to break down during competition. Without technical efficiency, athletes rarely zone.

2 **Be in Terrific Physical Shape:** Zoning usually stops when athletes get tired (physically and/or mentally). Obviously fatigue, cramping, and injury make zoning next to impossible. See Appendix H [of Dr. Neff's book, *Entering the Zone*] for more on dealing with sport-related injuries.

3 **Understand and Practice High-Percentage Strategies:** No matter how great an athlete's technique and fitness level, if she consistently chooses risky strategies, she will not be able to easily get into the zone when competing against athletes who know how to take advantage of tactical errors.

4 **Prepare Properly:** Make sure you've taken care of your equipment, diet, sleep, practice, and pre-competition warmup. Practice visualization daily. See Appendix E [of Dr. Neff's book, *Entering the Zone*] for ideas on how better to use practice to prepare for competition.

During the Competition

1 **Stay in the Present:** I don't know of any athlete in the history of sport who has zoned while they were angry or nervous. I truly don't believe it's even possible. By definition, a zoning athlete performs automatically, has high confidence, visualizes clearly, and feels almost constant pleasure, regardless of outcome. It is impossible to feel pleasure while dwelling on past mistakes or worrying about future outcomes. Some players may continue to perform well while angry or nervous, but the highest level of performance — the zone — will not happen until negative emotion is eliminated.

2 **Keep Thoughts Positive and Helpful:** As soon as an athlete becomes self-critical and negative, they lose the zone. Confidence is the key, and positive, helpful thoughts keep confidence high.

3 **Use a Good Ritual:** It's rare to zone throughout an entire competition. The athletes who have done it are able to manage their downtimes extremely well. Most every sport has lapses in action. During these times, successful athletes control their eyes, stay relaxed, visualize ideal strategies, and remain present to their thoughts. These rituals must be practiced so they too become automatic. For more ideas on rituals, see Appendix D [of Dr. Neff's book, *Entering the Zone*].

4 **"Flash" Visualize:** Just as you're about to execute a skill, imagine it in its ideal form. Some examples include: imagining where the ball will go on a tennis shot just prior to contact; imagining the trajectory of a jump shot just prior to shooting; imagining a move during a gymnastics floor routine just prior to executing it; imagining a one-on-one move in basketball just prior to doing it. Great athletes get a flash image of what they are going to do, and then they simply copy what they have just seen in their mind. This kind of visualizing can and must be practiced regularly before it will work consistently in competition.

Trying Without Caring

You might think trying and caring are *both* necessary for top performance, since few would try if they didn't care. However, I believe that they *cannot* both be present in athletes during zone performances, and here's why. Trying reflects the amount of physical and mental effort put forth during competition. Trying is obviously important to every athlete and coach. But caring is wishing for or wanting a specific future outcome, and future thinking during competition is what creates nervousness. So caring about the outcome or what people might think *destroys* the chance of zoning!

Most athletes I meet can't imagine competing without caring about the outcome. They really struggle with letting go and being okay with whatever result happens. Here's a sentence you can memorize to help with this issue: "As long as I ride hard, stay mentally calm, and problem solve throughout the race, I know I'm doing everything I can in the moment and the outcome will be what it is."

What we know about athletes in the zone is that they are so wrapped up in the moment, so focused on performance, that they are not consciously aware of consequences. In other words, in the moment of performing their skill, they do not care about what might or might not happen. Are they giving everything they have? Definitely! They may think about winning during breaks in action, but during the performance, in the middle of a zone experience, athletes simply don't care what might happen! So how do athletes get to this place of trying without caring?

Fortunately, we humans can only think of one thing at a time. That fact is what will save us all from under-performing or choking in our next big competition. All we have to do is recognize the future thought (maybe a sentence starting with "What if...") and insert another thought or picture. This simple solution is not always easy, especially if you are emotional or have a habit of trying not to blow it when things get tight. The key is to create a new habit of recognizing the future thought and exchanging it for a present thought or picture.

What does it look like when someone is trying hard but doesn't care about the outcome? He might be someone who isn't supposed to win. He might not have any expectations of what should happen in the competition. He might be someone who really loves competition (and just enjoys participating), or he might be someone who is focused on overcoming a mild injury (many people play their best when their thoughts are on how to get through a little pain). Whatever the underlying situation, his performance looks great! He is sharp, focused, relaxed, smiles often, is clearly having a good time, and is performing his best!

Here are some ideas on how to achieve the trying-without-caring state of mind:

1 **Recognize Future Thoughts:** Future thoughts are the ones that create feelings of importance and pressure. If these kinds of thoughts know they're not welcome, they won't come around too often. In order to get rid of them, you have to consistently exchange them for strategy thoughts.

2 **Smile Often:** Enjoy the experience. Not only will it feel better, but you'll perform better, too. As the Chinese proverb goes, "Happiness is not a state to arrive at, but a manner of traveling."

3 **Act As If:** Do what people who love to compete would do. They'd lay it all on the line and courageously battle throughout. They'd go for their shots. See Appendix F [of Dr. Neff's book, *Entering the Zone*] for more about champions.

4 **Compete Like an Underdog:** Underdogs don't choke — they usually raise their level of play. Choose to do all the things an underdog does.

5 **It Is What It Is:** Look at occurrences for what they actually are, not what you *think* they are. A flat tire doesn't mean you're destined to lose. It simply means you need to change a flat. Move on after mistakes without attaching meaning to outcomes.

The following interview with a professional tennis player is an example of what can happen when an athlete cares less about the outcome during competition. This athlete became so frustrated that at one point he said to himself, "Forget this tournament." But he's so passionate about the game that he couldn't stop trying, even though he chose not to care any more about the outcome. The result? Trying without caring enabled him to play better — and he actually won!

> May 25, 2004 — PARIS (AP) — Vince Spadea's comeback started when he stopped caring about winning. The American overcame nine match points and a 5-1 deficit in the fifth set Monday to beat French qualifier Florent Serra 7-5, 1-6, 4-6, 7-6 (7), 9-7.
>
> Spadea said he began taking risky swings when he found himself on the verge of defeat. "I was like, just give it away. Forget this tournament," he said. "And everything went in."
>
> Serra held so many match points in the 4 ½ hour marathon that Spadea lost track. "I think he had about five or six," Spadea said. Instead, Spadea survived one match point trailing 7-6 in the tiebreaker. He overcame three serving at 5-3 in the final set, then erased five more in the next game to make the score 5-all.
>
> Spadea, seeded 27th, converted his first match-point chance. "I'm a passionate guy about what I'm trying to accomplish," he said. "I just couldn't give up."

NOTE: If you're not trying *and* don't care, you may be burned out or overtrained. See the section later in this chapter called Athletic Burnout (The Opposite of Being In the Zone) for information on how to recognize and treat overtraining.

A NEW MODEL OF HOW TO FIND THE ZONE DURING PERFORMANCE

The Emotion Wheel

This flow diagram shows the process by which athletes can learn to control their emotions and find the zone during competition. The letters on the next page refer to the letters in the diagram.

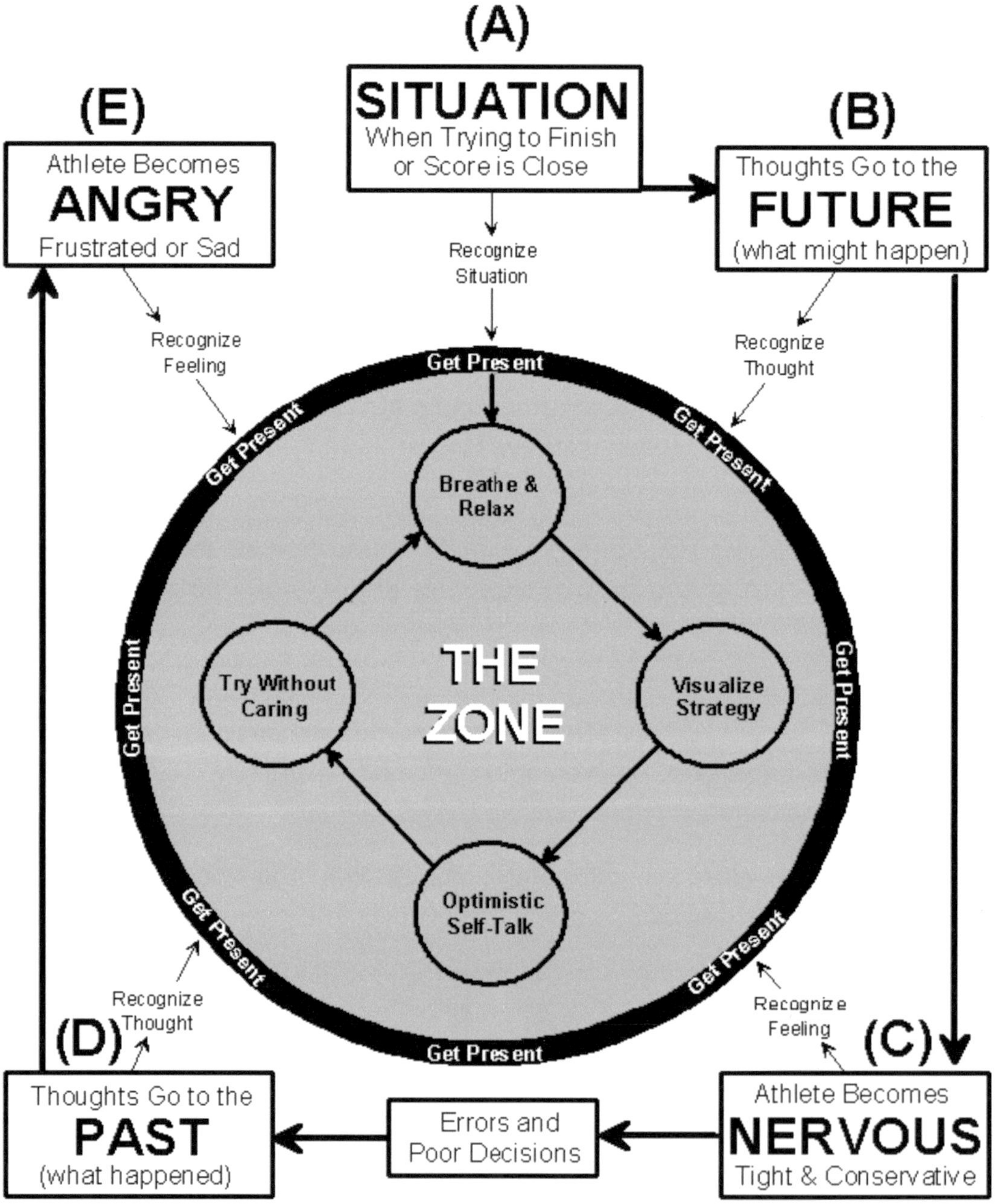

Diagram © Robert Neff, Ph.D.

A The process begins when the score gets close or when an athlete is trying to finish a competition.

B The athlete tends to think about the future and possible outcomes (what might happen).

C If that happens, the athlete will likely feel nervous, tight, and/or conservative. This type of feeling typically leads to errors and poor decisions.

D If too many errors occur, thoughts tend to stay in the past.

E Past thoughts trigger anger, frustration or sadness.

At any of these five stages, the solution is the same — to get present by simply recognizing the feeling, thought, or situation. The ideal path is from (A) to "Recognize Situation" to "Get Present" so nervousness and anger aren't experienced at all. Once present, the athlete can then breathe and relax, visualize an ideal strategy, use optimistic self-talk, and try without caring about the outcome. The success wheel begins to spin. The Zone stops when thoughts venture outside the circle. By memorizing The Emotion Wheel, athletes can learn to consciously enhance their performance during competition.

Exercise H: Describe a zone experience you've had in the past.

Start by giving it a title like "U.S. Open 2nd Round." This title will serve to jog your mind. Attach your opponent's name if appropriate. Describe how you felt during the zone. Talk about your confidence level, your emotions, your energy level, how you handled mistakes, and how long the zone lasted. Describe your state of being, whether you were aggressive or passive, loud or quiet, fast or slow, tight or loose. List any significant things you did to prepare that may have created this great performance. List any other things that you know consistently help you to find the zone.

Title: ______________________________________

How I Felt:

My Confidence, Emotions and Energy:

My Behavior and State of Being:

How I Should Prepare:

"In golf as in life, it is the follow-through that makes the difference."
— Proverb

JOURNEY'S END

We hope the information in this chapter has been helpful and inspiring as you journey toward your highest performance dreams. As with all "self-help" information, it is only really beneficial if it is incorporated into day-to-day routines.

We have created a special website to assist you with using this information. To access this site, go to www.roadmaptothezone.com and click on the Member Site link. The username and password are both "athlete".

We wish you all the success you deserve!

"It is good to have an end to journey toward, but it is the journey that matters in the end."
— Ursula LeGuin

NOTE: See the *Single-Step Motivational Software* description at the end of this chapter. You can download a free trial and use it to more quickly reach the goals you just created.

ATHLETIC BURNOUT (THE OPPOSITE OF BEING IN THE ZONE)

Physical Signs: Feelings of exhaustion, a lingering cold, frequent gastrointestinal problems (stomach ache), frequent headaches, sleeplessness, shortness of breath, strange weight loss.

Behavioral Signs: Quick temper, instantaneous frustration, feeling overburdened (first thought of the day is, "Oh, no!"), inability to hold feelings in, yelling, screaming, feelings of helplessness, giving up easily, loss of care for loved ones, greater risk-taking behavior, consistently decreased performances.

Sport-Related Signs: Reduced feel for the skill or movement, constant unhappiness with performance, always expecting bad performance, slower reactions, increased unforced errors over many competitions, difficulty focusing (poor concentration/eye control), treating coach and teammates like strangers, general impatience.

Ideal Candidate for Burnout: A dedicated overachiever with an external locus of control (does things for other people or for extrinsic rewards) or a person with extreme role conflict or role ambiguity (doesn't understand herself or how she fits into a variety of situations) [Fender (1989), Athlete burnout, The Sport Psychologist, 3 (1), pp. 63-71].

Burnout Avoidance

1 Become more aware of the symptoms and underlying causes of each.

2 Cross training (use other related sports to help accomplish fitness goals).

3 Day(s) off (proper periodization training should include days off).

4 Change of scenery (different practice location, inside vs. outside, road trips).

5 Support from others (friends, family, coach, sport psychologist).

6 Work with a sport psychologist.

7 Tournament scheduling (allow time to rest and recover).

8 Practice scheduling (quality, not just quantity).

9 Proper goal setting (focus only on things you control).

ABOUT THE SINGLE-STEP MOTIVATIONAL SOFTWARE

I've included information about motivational software because I think it can significantly help you stick to your action lists and achieve your highest dreams. Once you have the software loaded and set up, you'll be able to take the Roadmap and Action Lists you've created in this chapter and enter them directly into the software. You can then sit back and let the software keep you on track. Below is a list of features and a description of how to install and use the software.

Features

- Allows you to define your life as you see it currently.
- Allows you to identify the areas you would most like to change.
- Helps you define your goals.
- Helps you progress daily towards your goals and notice the progress that you are making.
- Helps you chart and plan new goals as old goals are achieved.
- Helps you motivate yourself, providing daily inspiration as needed to help you past those low moments.
- Provides a method to help convince your sub-conscious of your commitment to your goal, and of the need to change.
- Provides encouragement as you progress along the path.

How to Use the Software

1 Install and set up the software, which uses cutting-edge psychological techniques to improve success by activating the Limbic System in the brain.

2 Complete daily exercises involving setting goals, visualization, and positive self-talk (affirmations). Exercises take approximately 15-30 minutes a day and should be done consistently for visualization to become a habit. As each exercise is completed, the software will provide you with a score for feedback and motivation.

3 As you reach your goals, be sure to add new goals and supporting steps from your Roadmap.

Installation and Setup

1 Download the software onto a PC with an internet connection (there is no Mac edition yet). There is a free trial period that enables you to become familiar with the system. The website is www.single-step.com/roadmap/offer.html.

2 Install the software. If you purchased it, enter a registration code to unlock all the features.

3 Launch the software and complete the Self-Description Wizard (it will come up automatically when you first open the software). Three more wizards will automatically run – one after another – to guide you through the steps. You can manually start them from the Wizards menu if you want to change the information later.

4 Complete the Goal Definition Wizard. Enter the goals you created using the flow charts and action lists. If the software moves you to the next wizard before you've entered your goals, you can always return to the Goal Definition Wizard later to finish later.

5 Complete the Image Locator Wizard by downloading pictures from the internet that will inspire you to reach your specific goals.

6 Complete the Affirmation Definition Wizard by typing in one statement for each of your goals. These are statements the software will ask you to repeat to yourself 15 times a day. They need to be positive, optimistic statements.

7 Assign your affirmations to your images. When you repeat your affirmations, the software will show display your images at the same time. This is a powerful feature.

8 Open the Visualization Wizard from the Wizards menu. Follow the directions to create a visualization sequence to rehearse for each goal.

9 Make sure each goal has a contemplation statement – an idealistic image or thought related to your goal (i.e.: How would it change my life if I graduated at the top of my class?).

I wish you all the best in achieving your cycling goals!

About the Author

Robert S. Neff, Ph.D., is a former multi-sport college varsity athlete who later competed on the professional tennis tour. He earned his Ph.D. in sport psychology from the Department of Kinesiology at Michigan State University and is the past president of the Association of Applied Sport Psychology Professionals (AASPP). As a college professor, Dr. Neff teaches sport psychology courses and consults privately in the Dallas area with athletes of all sports. He has made it his career mission to simplify sport psychology concepts so athletes and coaches can more effectively use them in their training and competitions. Dr. Neff's newest book, *Roadmap to the Zone: Enhancing Athletic Performance*, is in bookstores now. You can contact Dr. Neff at www.robertneff.com.

The following is Chapter 1 from Nutrition for the Long Run *by sport dietician Heidi Smith, R.D. You can find out more about improving performance, developing lifelong healthy eating habits, and author Heidi Smith at* www.heidismithnutrition.com.

EATING FOR ENERGY

The Importance of Nutrition as a Foundation for Training

The foods you choose on a daily basis have a profound impact on your health, your energy, and your performance in sports. The better you fuel your body, the more energy your muscles can store, the faster you recover, and the harder you can train. Your fuel determines your athletic potential. Food is the foundation of your training.

Food as Fuel

Your body derives energy from three main food sources: carbohydrates, protein, and fat. In general, carbohydrates are your main fuel for exercise, proteins are the building blocks for muscle, and fats provide a concentrated source of energy. Finding the proper balance of these main nutrients is the key to increased energy, longer endurance, and faster recovery.

To better understand the role of these nutrients, think of your body as a high-performance car. Carbohydrates are the high-octane fuel. Carbs are an efficient fuel source, burning clean and fast. You have to keep your fuel tank topped up at all times to avoid running out of gas, so you should consume carbohydrates regularly throughout the day. Spend a little extra time and effort to get high-quality fuel by choosing complex carbohydrates that are less refined, such as whole wheat breads, pastas, and brown rice.

Protein is analogous to your car's engine. You need regular amounts of protein each day to facilitate repairs, particularly muscle repair after a hard workout. Unlike carbohydrates, protein is not burned as a main fuel, so you don't need to eat large quantities. You also need a small amount of high-quality fat in your diet — like the oil in your car — to keep everything running smoothly. To complete the analogy, think of water as your coolant. Without adequate water, your engine will overheat, and you will be forced to cool off at the side of the road.

ACHIEVING THE RIGHT BALANCE

In scientific terms, individuals who exercise need to get a minimum of 55-65% of their calories from carbohydrates, 12-15% from protein, and 20-25% from fat. When serving up your dinner meal, percentages of nutrients may be hard to measure. One method to achieve the right balance is to aim for a dinner plate that is ¾ carbohydrates (vegetables, grains, fruits) and ¼ protein (meats, beans, soy, dairy). Even though this looks like 75% carbohydrates, carb sources are bulkier and also contain some protein, so it actually comes out close to the recommended percentages. Refer to Chapter 3 [of Smith's book, *Nutrition for the Long Run*] for more details on meal timing, balance, and portions.

Another useful tool is *Canada's Food Guide to Healthy Eating*. Although it was developed for the general public, the principles are still applicable to athletes. It advocates choosing whole grain and enriched carbohydrates, emphasizing dark green and orange vegetables, and choosing lower-fat dairy and leaner protein sources. The recommended food servings provide approximately 1800-3200 calories with a balance of 55% carbohydrates, 15% protein, and less than 30% fat. Some athletes will require additional servings of all the food groups to meet their energy requirements. Refer to Appendix D [of Smith's book, *Nutrition for the Long Run*] for details on how to get guidance on setting up an eating plan specifically for you.

Carbohydrate, Glycogen, and Endurance

Carbohydrates come from any food that is starchy or sweet. Main sources include grains, breads, pastas, fruits, vegetables, and to a lesser extent, dairy products. When carbs are consumed they are broken down and stored in the body as glycogen. Glycogen is simply the technical name for stored carbohydrates. Glycogen is stored mainly in the liver (used for blood sugar control) and muscles (used as fuel for exercise). In fact, it is one of the only fuels we can burn during anaerobic exercise. Anaerobic exercise can be defined as working at a pace where it is difficult to talk without gasping for air. In other words, if you are out of breath or working at a high intensity, your main fuel is glycogen. Even in low- to moderate-intensity exercise such as walking or marathon running, glycogen is still the limiting fuel. If you run out of glycogen during a workout, you will hit the wall and have to stop.

Think of glycogen as the wick in a candle and your fat stores as the wax. If you have no glycogen you cannot sustain a flame, and therefore you can't burn energy – even if you have a lot of stored fat available. As in a candle, our glycogen stores (the wick) are very small in comparison to our fat stores (the wax). Our glycogen stores alone can only sustain high-intensity exercise for about 90 minutes. Theoretically, if we use only our fat stores for energy, we could run four marathons in a row! Unfortunately, fat can only be burned in aerobic conditions, and only in the presence of a small amount of glycogen. So we come back to carbohydrates – and glycogen – as the limiting factor for endurance exercise.

One last point to consider is the ability for glycogen to recover after a workout. If you are exercising for more than 90 minutes, you are depleting your glycogen stores. Keep in mind that glycogen takes

24-48 hours to fully replenish, even for someone on a high-carbohydrate diet. Refer to the Eating after Exercise section later in this chapter for tips on speeding up recovery.

Glycogen Summary

- It is the storage form of carbohydrate.
- It is the limiting fuel for endurance exercise.
- It is needed to burn fat.
- We have a limited capacity to store it.
- It recovers slowly.
- Athletes need to eat a high-carbohydrate diet.

EATING BEFORE EXERCISE

The purpose of a pre-exercise snack is to help maintain your blood sugar until the exercise starts. Carbohydrates from a pre-exercise snack are broken down and absorbed into the blood stream as sugar. The body regulates blood sugar very closely because it is the main fuel used by the brain. If blood sugar drops, the brain will trigger a breakdown of glycogen (muscle fuel) and possibly steal essential energy from your muscles. To optimize energy for your workout, aim for a small meal or snack two to three hours before you exercise. This snack should provide a short-term energy boost to prevent blood sugar from dropping.

The pre-exercise snack does not provide fuel for your workout. Remember from the previous section that it takes 24-48 hours for muscle fuel (glycogen) to store and become available to burn. Therefore, you are not burning your pre-workout snack during a workout — you are burning what you ate and stored one to two days earlier. That is why you can get away with a very light snack before a long, hard workout. Some athletes even prefer drinking just a glass of water before exercising first thing in the morning.

The early morning is an exception to the two- to three-hour pre-exercise eating recommendation. Contrary to other times of day, blood sugars can be quite stable upon waking in the morning. If you prefer to exercise on an empty stomach, try a small glass of juice, a piece of toast, or even some sport drink 15-30 minutes before exercise. This small amount of easily digested carbohydrates will help raise your blood sugar enough for you to start your workout feeling energized. Once again, it's not the fuel in your stomach that counts, it's the fuel that's stored in your muscle and circulating as blood sugar.

The pre-exercise snack can take many forms, depending on what time you exercise and what works best for you. Some guidelines for choosing food before exercise follow.

Pre-Exercise Eating Guidelines

Choose foods high in carbohydrates, moderate in fiber, and low in sugar.

Carbohydrates are the main nutrient that keeps your blood sugar stable before exercise. High-fiber carbohydrates (more than five grams of fiber per serving) add bulk to your meal and leave you feeling full. Fullness is a good thing most of the time, but two to three hours before exercise you want food to clear quickly from your stomach.

Be cautious with sweet carbohydrates. They have a high glycemic index, which means they are absorbed very quickly, contributing to a fast rise and crash in blood sugar levels. A sugar high even 30 minutes before exercise may leave you feeling tired and sluggish at the beginning of your workout.

Examples of low-sugar, moderate-fiber carbohydrates include whole grain products like breads, pitas, low-fat/low-sugar homemade muffins, cold cereals (low in sugar), and warm cereals like oatmeal, bagels, pasta, potatoes, and fruits.

Your pre-exercise meal should contain some protein if eaten more than two hours before exercise.

Protein slows the absorption of carbohydrates to help maintain a constant blood sugar level. Choose lower fat protein sources to promote faster digestion. Since protein is digested more slowly than carbohydrates, limit protein intake as you approach exercise time (see Figure 11-A).

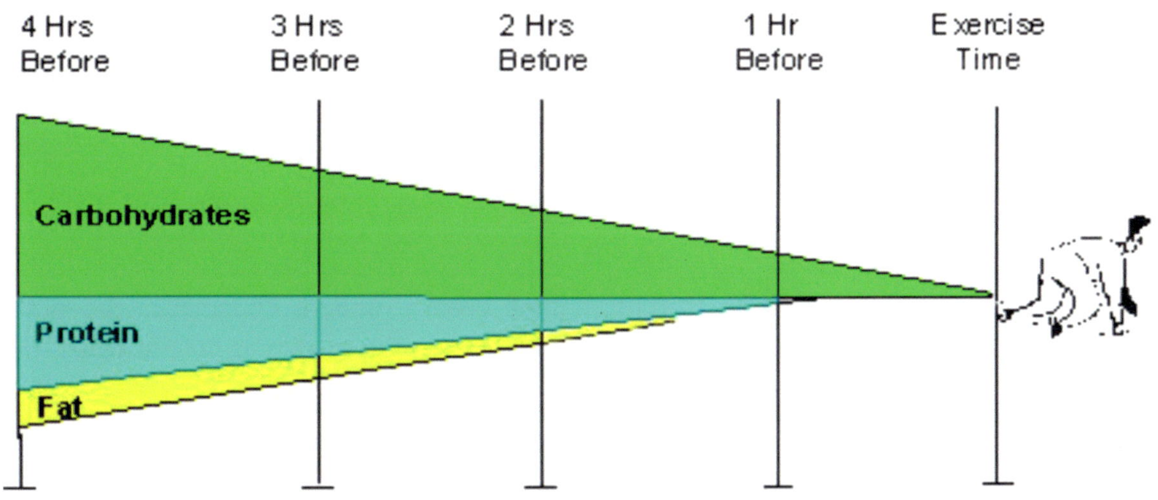

Figure 11-A

Examples of low-fat protein sources include lean cuts of sandwich meats (turkey or chicken breast, roast beef, ham), light peanut butter, fish (tuna canned in water, varieties like sole or cod), eggs, and low-fat dairy or soy products (<20% milkfat cheese, 1-2% milkfat yogurt, skim or 1% milk).

Your pre-meal three to four hours before exercise can include carbohydrate with some protein and fat. As you near the time of exercise, the size of the meal/snack should decrease and the selection should be primarily carbohydrates with minimal fat and protein.

Choose low-fat foods.

Fats slow digestion and may lead to discomfort if eaten too close to exercise. Depending on the size of your pre-exercise meal, limit the total fat intake to about 10-20 grams. See Chapter 5 [of Smith's book, *Nutrition for the Long Run*] for some low-fat choices at restaurants. Limit fat as you get closer to your exercise time. Examples of high-fat foods to limit include: regular-fat cheeses, nuts, sauces, gravies, butter, margarine, fried foods, croissants, and baked goods.

Choose foods with which you are familiar and comfortable.

Avoid trying new foods right before a workout. In particular, avoid heavily spiced foods such as hot peppers, garlic, and onions. These foods can lead to stomach upset and discomfort during exercise. Trial and error will help you determine what's best for you.

Maintain adequate fluids throughout the day.

Fluids are a major key to a successful workout. Be sure you are well-hydrated before, during, and after exercise. Drink about two cups of fluid 30-60 minutes before you exercise. This will assist your stomach in emptying during exercise, and it will help prevent cramping. Avoid drinks that contain alcohol and caffeine, as they can contribute to dehydration.

Pre-Exercise Foods to Avoid

1 **High in Sugar:** sugary cereals, candy, candy bars, ice cream, soft drinks

2 **High in Dietary Fiber:** beans of any kind, prunes, gassy vegetables (broccoli, onions, cauliflower, brussel sprouts)

3 **High in Fat:** full-fat dairy products (cheese, ice cream, milks), chocolate, chocolate bars, high-fat meats (chicken wings, sausages), anything deep-fried such as potato chips

4 **Fast Food:** cheeseburgers, hotdogs, tacos, wings, greasy pizzas, french fries

Pre-Exercise Snack Ideas

Ideally, aim for a snack two to three hours before exercise. However, if you must eat fewer than two hours before exercising, Figure 11-B contains some sample snack ideas.

TIME BEFORE EXERCISE	COMPOSITION	FOOD IDEAS
2-4 Hours Prior	Balanced Meal or Snack	Sandwich with low fat toppings, cheese and fruit, trail mix, peanut butter and crackers, soup and salad, pasta with meat sauce, French toast, egg on toast, pizza with low-fat cheese (hold the pepperoni).
1-2 Hours Prior	High-Carb Moderate-Protein Low-Fat	Cereal with skim milk, low-fat yogourt and fruit, sport bar (<10 grams of protein), yogurt shake.
<1 Hour Prior	High-Carb Low-Protein Low-Fat	Crackers, sport drink, fruit, toast, half or whole bagel with cream cheese, sport bar (less than 10 grams of protein).

Figure 11-B

EATING DURING EXERCISE: INCREASING ENDURANCE

The most effective way to spare glycogen stores and increase endurance is to consume carbohydrates during exercise lasting longer than 90 minutes. Most of us have enough glycogen to keep our flame burning for about one and a half hours of continuous high intensity exercise. However, after 90 minutes without a source of carbohydrate from food or drink, complete exhaustion is just around the corner.

Complete exhaustion is also known as "bonking" or "hitting the wall" – a very unpleasant experience where you are physically unable to continue exercising. To avoid hitting the wall, consume .7-1 gram of carbohydrates per kilogram of body weight per hour during exercise. This works out to about 30-60 grams of carbohydrate per hour of exercise. You should start consuming carbohydrates after the first 60-90 minutes.

Carbohydrates are the only fuel your body needs during exercise. Therefore, seek food and drink sources low in protein or fat. Popular sources include sport drinks, bars, and gels. See Chapter 6 [of Smith's book, *Nutrition for the Long Run*] for a comparison of different products. Supplements are convenient and usually designed for easy digestion, however, good, old-fashioned food can produce equal results. Figure 11-C shows some common foods used during exercise.

Guidelines for Choosing Food to Consume During Exercise

- Look for carbohydrates that are low in fiber (less than grams of fiber per serving). Fiber is essential in your regular diet, but it is too slow to digest during exercise.
- For high-intensity exercise (more than 60% of your max), avoid fats and protein since they will also slow digestion (less than five grams of protein or fat per serving).
- Consider how convenient the food is to carry and eat while exercising.
- Be sure to consume a minimum of two to four cups of fluid with any solid food you choose. Consuming food without adequate fluid can cause stomach upset and indigestion.
- Consume foods in small amounts over the hour rather than all at once.
- Try a food several times during training to be sure it works for you before trying it in a race.

Common Foods Used During Exercise

Keep in mind the recommendation of 40-60 grams of carbohydrates per hour of exercise.

FOOD	SERVING SIZE	CALORIES (kCal)	CARBS (g)	SODIUM (mg)	FIBER (g)	PROTEIN (g)	FAT (g)
Bagel (plain)	1 (110 g)	302	59	587	2.5	11.5	2
Banana (medium)	1 (190 g)	108	28	1.2	2.8	1.2	0.6
Raisins	¼ cup	124	33	5	1.6	1.3	0.2
Dried Apricots	¼ cup	79	20	3	3	1.2	0.2
Arrowroots	4 (20 g)	88	14	74	0.04	1.6	2.8
Baked Potato	1 (172 g)	188	43.5	14	4	4.0	0.4
Saltines	10	118	20	356	0.8	3.0	2.8
Pretzels (low-fat)	12	100	23	400	0.9	3.0	2.1
Graham Crackers	4 (28 g)	119	21	185	0.9	2.0	2.8
Fat-Free Fig Bars	4	260	62	244	1.6	2.0	0.4
Granola Bar (low-fat)	1 (26 g)	110	20	40	1.2	1.1	2.5
Homemade Sport Drink (water with five tsp honey and 1/8 tsp salt)	500 ml	100	25	250	0	0	0

Figure 11-C

Three Easy Steps for a Workout Eating Plan

Here is an example of how to use a combination of foods, fluids, and supplements during a three-hour workout.

1 Calculate your carbohydrate needs based on .7-1 gram of carbohydrates per kilogram of body weight per hour. For example, a 70 kg athlete would need 50-70 grams of carbohydrates per hour after the first hour of exercise.

2 Choose a combination of food and/or fluid that appeals to you. For example: pretzels, Gatorade sport drink, Powerbar sport bar.

3 Using the tables of carbohydrate values provided, plan out the quantities needed and the timing. Remember, for best absorption it is best to spread out your consumption of carbohydrates over the hour.

Hour 1: 500-750 ml water

Hour 2: 500 ml Gatorade (28 grams of carbs),
12 Pretzels (23 grams of carbs) (eat three every 15 minutes)

Hour 3: 250 ml water, 250 ml Gatorade (14 grams of carbs),
One Powerbar (45 grams of carbs) (eat ¼ of the bar every 15 minutes)

EATING AFTER EXERCISE: FASTER RECOVERY

After a hard workout, your glycogen stores will be depleted, you may be dehydrated, and your muscles will need some time to repair and rebuild. The body needs 24-48 hours to fully replenish glycogen stores after an endurance workout. If you are working out every other day, recovery may not be a problem. Your regular high-carbohydrate diet will help to restore your fuel tank of glycogen in due time.

However, many athletes train every day, sometimes several times per day. In these cases, fast recovery can be critical to keep pace with a busy training schedule. One of the most effective ways to increase recovery time is to eat immediately after a workout.

There is a recovery window of two hours following a workout. During this period your muscles are in overdrive trying to repair and replenish. A snack within 15-30 minutes after exercise provides the fastest recovery. If you can provide the right fuel soon after exercise, you can double the speed of glycogen recovery.

This can be an incredible performance-enhancing tool because you can maximize your energy stores in a shorter amount of time. That means you'll be ready for your next workout sooner. Use the following tips to make the best use of your recovery window.

Eating Tips for Faster Recovery from Exercise

1. Consume a high-carbohydrate, moderate-protein snack immediately after your workout, preferably within 15-30 minutes. See Figure 11-D for some ideas.
2. The post-workout snack should contain a minimum of 50 grams of carbohydrates along with a source of protein (7-15 grams should be adequate). A small amount of protein may help the muscle repair faster. Larger amounts of carbohydrates are needed because this is the fuel that has been burned. Simply consuming a normal high-carb training diet composed of frequent small meals and snacks every two to three hours will help achieve glycogen recovery. See Chapter 3 [of Smith's book, *Nutrition for the Long Run*] for tips on meal timing and balance to ensure constant recovery throughout your day.
3. Drink enough water during your workouts to maintain your weight. Maintaining your weight ensures that you're balancing sweat loss. Staying adequately hydrated will help your circulation carry lactic acid and waste products away from the muscle. Lactic acid is one of the culprits in muscle soreness after exercise. Appendix F [of Smith's book, *Nutrition for the Long Run*] has a weight log to help you track your level of hydration before and after exercise. Chapter 2 [of Smith's book, *Nutrition for the Long Run*] also has detailed tips for adequate hydration.
4. Take at least one recovery day per week. Adequate recovery time can be as essential as adequate training time. Allow at least one full day for your muscles to completely refuel and repair.

Post-Workout Snack Ideas

SNACK	CALORIES (kCal)	CARBS (g)	PROTEIN (g)
Two cups chocolate milk (made with 1% milk or soymilk)	340	56	17
Two cups chocolate milk (made with skim milk powder)	278	50	18
One liter (four cups) 6-8% carbohydrate sport drink	224	56	0
One cup milk (or soymilk), 1¼ cup cereal (i.e., Vector)	275	53	13
One banana, low-fat yogurt (175 ml)	250	48	13
Peanut butter and jam sandwich	350	50	12
300 ml Sunny Orange Shake	278	51	11
One cup trail mix made with dried fruit and cereal	280	40	15

Figure 11-D

Appendix A: ABOUT THE AUTHOR

Coach Richard P. Wharton owns and operates Online Bike Coach (www.onlinebikecoach.com), an online and on-site coaching, training, and testing business based in Dallas, Texas. He has been coaching since 1993, and is currently a Category 3 road cyclist.

Richard began cycling in the late 1980s. In the 1990s, he lived in Montana and Idaho, where he operated a junior development program and was an expert-level mountain biker. He returned to Dallas in 1999 to work on the Dallas 2012 Olympic Bid, and in 2000 he became Director of Development at the Superdrome in Frisco. In 2002 he interned at Tailwind Sports, which at the time owned and operated the US Postal Service Pro Cycling Team.

Richard is accompanied in life by his wife, Amy, and their Boston terrier, Shadow. His custom vanity Lance Armstrong license plate reads simply: "POWER".

Appendix B: COMPUTRAINER COACHING SOFTWARE FLOWCHART

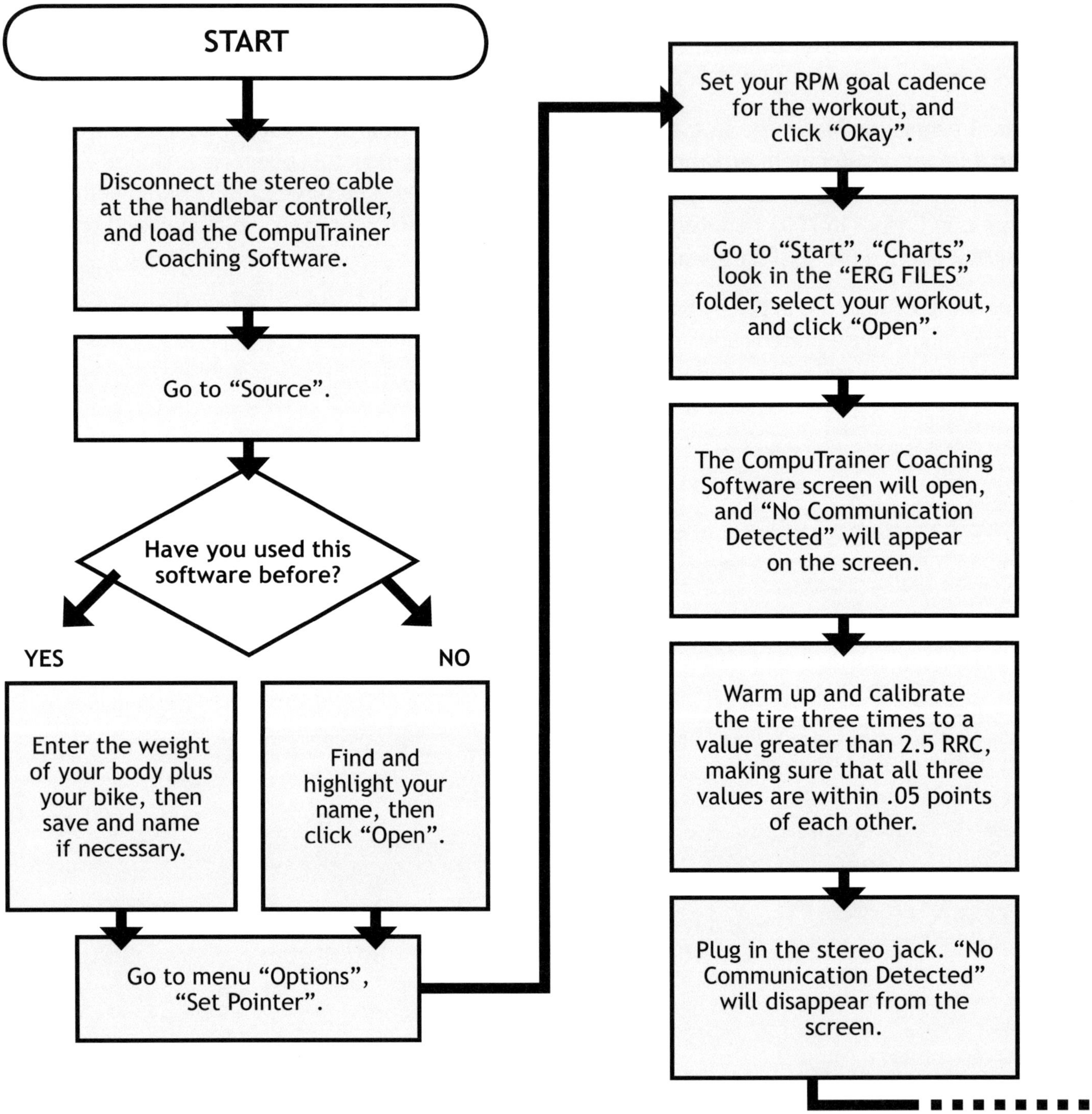

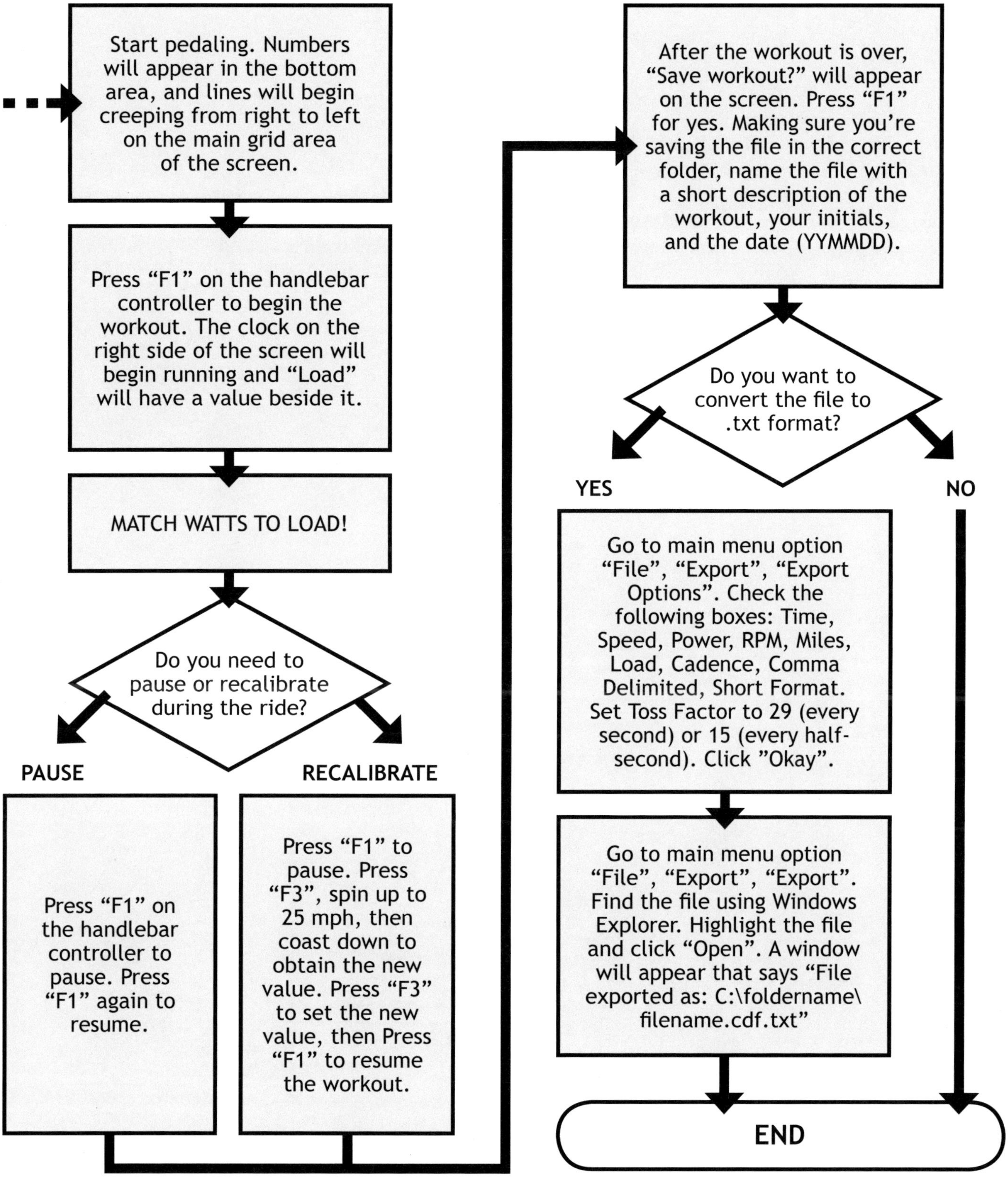
Start pedaling. Numbers will appear in the bottom area, and lines will begin creeping from right to left on the main grid area of the screen.
Press "F1" on the handlebar controller to begin the workout. The clock on the right side of the screen will begin running and "Load" will have a value beside it.
MATCH WATTS TO LOAD!
Do you need to pause or recalibrate during the ride?
PAUSE
RECALIBRATE
Press "F1" on the handlebar controller to pause. Press "F1" again to resume.
Press "F1" to pause. Press "F3", spin up to 25 mph, then coast down to obtain the new value. Press "F3" to set the new value, then Press "F1" to resume the workout.
After the workout is over, "Save workout?" will appear on the screen. Press "F1" for yes. Making sure you're saving the file in the correct folder, name the file with a short description of the workout, your initials, and the date (YYMMDD).
Do you want to convert the file to .txt format?
YES
NO
Go to main menu option "File", "Export", "Export Options". Check the following boxes: Time, Speed, Power, RPM, Miles, Load, Cadence, Comma Delimited, Short Format. Set Toss Factor to 29 (every second) or 15 (every half-second). Click "Okay".
Go to main menu option "File", "Export", "Export". Find the file using Windows Explorer. Highlight the file and click "Open". A window will appear that says "File exported as: C:\foldername\filename.cdf.txt"
END

$21.00
ISBN-10: 0-615-31505-4
ISBN-13: 978-0-615-31505-8
52100>
9 780615 315058

Made in the USA
Monee, IL
12 September 2026

62979101R00062